Rewriting My Happily Ever After

A Memoir of Divorce and Discovery

൹

Dr. Ranjani Rao

Rewriting My Happily Ever After © Dr. Ranjani Rao 2021

All rights reserved. No part of this publication may be reproduced, stored in a retrieval system, or transmitted in any form or by any means, electronic, mechanical, photocopying, recording or otherwise, without the prior written permission of the author. The only exception is brief quotations in printed reviews.

Dr. Ranjani Rao asserts the moral right to be identified as the **author of this work.**

Rewriting My Happily Ever After is a work of nonfiction. Some names and identifying details have been changed.

E-ISBN - 978-1-7340631-8-9
P-ISBN - 978-1-7340631-9-6

Book cover design by **Angelia Gan.**

Book layout by **Subramanian Ganga Devi.**

For information, contact the author at
www.ranjanirao.com

Published by Story Artisan Press
www.storyartisan.com

To Amma and Dada

Contents

Preface   *i*

Prologue   *iii*

I - FALLING

Leaving	3
Facing my fears	5
Making a list	12
Asking for a hug	17
Money matters	21

II - STARTING OVER

Coming home	29
Requesting help	33
Seeking solace	37
Expressing myself	42
Books matter	48
Don't judge	53
Walking therapy	59
Eating well	63
Returning to Yoga	70
Carrying on	75
Prioritizing self-care	80

Prevailing, again	83
Attitude of gratitude	88
Helping others	95
Avoiding negativity	98
Accepting invitations	101
Finding beauty	107
Chasing motherhood	111
Dodging depression	118

III - MAKING IT WORK

Excavating the real me	125
Going with the flow	130
Laughing	133
Exploring new talents	136
Small wins	143
Celebrating a birthday	148
Working with my strengths	152
Happy place	156
Writing my way out	161
Be a part of something larger	166
Getting away from it all	172
What will the parents say?	177
Forgiveness	181
No more doubts	188
Choosing to surrender	194

IV - RECONFIGURING LIFE

One small change — 201

Collaborate and create — 208

Giving back — 215

Creating connections — 220

Taking the driver's seat — 225

Moving toward meditation — 231

Growing up — 235

Marking anniversaries — 240

Embracing my single life — 245

V - SOARING

Owning my name — 253

Happy Days — 259

Incorporating rituals — 264

Grand gesture — 270

Also by Dr. Ranjani Rao — 276

About the author — 277

Acknowledgements — 278

Request — 279

You must understand the whole of life, not just one part of it. That is why you must read, that is why you must look at the skies, why you must sing, dance and write poems, and suffer, and understand, for all that is life.

~J. Krishnamurti

Preface

Telling the story of my divorce, of breaking the bonds of a long marriage that produced one child, is not easy.

Divorce is not unusual. The statistics, although evolving, are unequivocal. I've read that in the United States between forty and fifty percent of marriages end in divorce.

In India, the numbers are not so clear, partly because of poor record keeping but mostly because no one wants to talk about divorce, much less track it. Whether we measure it or refuse to admit it, the fact remains that divorce is becoming increasingly common. It is as much a part of our life as birth and death.

After sixteen years of marriage, I walked out of the home I shared with my husband with no idea what lay ahead—for me, my daughter, and our place in society. When I abandoned the script for my life that had been written for me, I was forced to forge a new path paved only with my own decisions.

I did not know anyone else in my inner circle who was divorced. There was no role model for me to emulate, no road map of how to tread on this new path. For the three years that followed my departure, I was lonely, scared, and full of doubts.

Was I the first to feel this way? Was I the only one who had experienced the grief and struggle that accompanies the dissolution of a long marriage? Though I asked these questions, I knew that I was neither the first nor the only one to experience divorce. Why then did I feel so lost?

I grew up in Mumbai and was raised in a family that valued education. I was bold, outspoken, and believed in gender equality. I completed my PhD on a scholarship, held a job for my entire adult life, and had lived abroad. Yet I stayed in my unhappy marriage for many years. Why?

For the same reasons that many Indian women do.

I did not have answers to the dreaded questions: What will people say? What will the parents say? What about the child(ren)? How will I manage alone?

I wrote this book to describe my process to figure out the answers to these questions as a way to help women who, like me, may find themselves hesitating on the brink of a decision about their marriage. To my surprise, through the catharsis and clarity that arises from writing, I found closure.

Throughout the book, I describe the tools and practices that shaped my life at a time when I was raw with hurt and disappointed—both at the world and myself.

Your story may be different, your route to getting to the point where you picked up this book may be more treacherous or less, but if you ever felt the need to know that you are not alone, this book is for you.

I fully believe that you too will be able to figure things out, find help from unexpected people, and most importantly, discover a reservoir of strength from the one source that you may not have considered—within yourself.

It is possible to walk the path we have been assigned with gratitude and forgiveness, courage and grace, humility and confidence, without falling apart.

I invite you to read this book and rewrite your happily ever after. Always remember this:

It is never too late - in fiction or in life - to revise
~ Nancy Thayer

Prologue

We know what we are but know not what we may be
~ William Shakespeare

The flyer on the notice board outside the gym caught my eye, not just for the pale blue background with its striking orange text, but for the title:

"So, you're thinking about divorce?" Had someone overheard my thoughts and created this poster?

The title was intriguing, specific about the subject but vague about the product. Was it a book? Or a seminar? Although eager to get back to the office after my lunchtime aerobics class, I stopped to read further.

It was a six-week workshop beginning the following week for people unsure about whether they wanted a divorce, and it was covered by our employee assistance program. When I returned to my desk that afternoon, I called and registered.

I was the ideal candidate. The workshop title perfectly reflected my ambivalence about divorce. On the surface, we were a successful Indian couple living in the San Francisco Bay area—dual income, one kid.

We had managed to stay married for over a decade, although it had been a long time since either of us could call it a happy marriage. It wasn't even peaceful, but it was what we had.

We had both accepted the unwritten rule of arranged marriage: love, if it arrived at all, would bloom with time.

Wasn't a decade long enough to wait for love to bloom? I wondered on the drive back home. Especially on days like this when I returned from work, dreading the hours I had to spend with a husband who was more of an annoying roommate than supportive spouse, yet looking forward to spending time with our small child whom we both loved.

Once you have a baby, everything will be fine.

I had heard that refrain enough times from relatives, friends, and strangers who believed that the purpose of marriage was procreation and that the objective of a child's life was to hold on to each parent and keep them together through a combination of guilt, love, duty, and fear.

Was a child enough of a glue to hold us together? She had arrived after much struggle and intervention, on both medical and spiritual fronts.

After we became parents, almost eight years after becoming husband and wife, things *were* different—for a while. We entered into a prolonged period of ceasefire during which we parked our frustrations behind the mountain of attention needed by our newborn daughter. Yet as she grew from infancy to toddlerhood and into a happy preschooler, my doubts continued to increase.

Shouldn't there be more to a marriage? A clarity of purpose? A unity of vision? Team spirit? Common goals? A mutual love of things and each other? We didn't seem to have any of these. In the three short weeks between our first meeting and wedding—typical of such weddings between an expat Indian boy and an India-based girl—had I missed a memo about how to make an arranged marriage work?

I hoped the workshop would help me clarify my thoughts about what I wanted from a marriage, if not an outright divorce.

※

At 6 p.m. on the following Wednesday, I joined a motley group of people in a small clinic in downtown Palo Alto. Eight people sat in chairs arranged in a circle—two couples, three women, and Linda, the facilitator, a middle-aged woman with short silver hair and bright red lipstick.

I was surprised to see couples. Clearly, both were thinking about divorce, as the workshop title suggested, or at least one was thinking about it and was able to convince their spouse to join the session. Interesting!

I had not broached the subject to anyone. The "D-word" was unmentionable. I had made some work-related excuse to my husband to attend the first session.

Linda went around the room and asked us to introduce ourselves and why we were there. Every person in the room had been married longer than me, all had children, but I was the only Indian.

The situation was not unusual. I had experienced something similar on the first day of orientation at my workplace, then at the Lamaze class at the hospital, and, most recently, at the weekly lunchtime aerobics session at the office gym. The superficial difference hadn't mattered in those situations, but now it did.

In fact, it was at the heart of the matter.

"How did you feel when you first met? Were there sparks? Do you remember the early feelings of being in love? The excitement, the passion?" Linda asked.

Instantly the energy of the room changed as everyone swung their attention to a more pleasant time in their lives, days suffused with the gentle flush of attraction and joyful anticipation.

Everyone responded. Some spoke eloquently about their courtship—the flamboyant wooing, the lavish gifts, the fancy meals. Others spoke of kind gestures and thoughtful words, of support during a minor illness and of romantic Christmas gatherings with both sides of the family. There was a wistful quality to their reminiscence; their expressions softened as they recollected the early days of infatuation and falling in love.

When my turn came, I was speechless.

How does one go about defending and defining an arranged marriage to a roomful of people unfamiliar with the custom?

"I had an arranged marriage," I said hesitantly, expecting the phrase to be self-explanatory.

A distant relative had suggested a suitable boy to my parents, who had dutifully contacted the boy's parents, and the rest, as they say, was history. When spoken aloud, the story sounded lame and archaic, and depending on the listener's awareness of the subject, it could be interpreted as either a quaint or regressive custom.

I didn't expect an average American to understand the social setup that not only encourages but also supports this system of matching people (and families) within similar socioeconomic and culturally homogenous groups, a practice based on the assumption that overlapping backgrounds and value systems lead to a more harmonious union.

In the West, most pop culture references to such marriages were stereotypical tropes of unfortunate women being forced into a marriage without consent, often agreeing to a match under pressure and always for reasons other than love.

It hadn't been that way for me. No one had held a gun to my head or emotionally blackmailed me into agreeing to the match. We were introduced under the supervision of parents at my home in Mumbai and spent some time talking, just the two of us. As a recent college graduate, I expressed my desire to attend graduate school without expressly stating it as a deal breaker if he disagreed. He graciously expressed support and we both said yes. And just like that, we were married.

Just as my agreement to marry a stranger seemed odd to Americans, despite the proclaimed longevity of Indian marriages, I was equally baffled by my young American classmates and colleagues who chose their partners without any involvement of their families.

A PhD candidate in my department married a man who drove a UPS truck for a living, whereas a scientist I worked with was seriously considering proposing to the ballerina he was dating. I marveled at their emphasis on "falling in love" and their confidence in marriage despite the statistics about divorce.

Although a trained marriage counselor, Linda seemed clueless about the mechanics of a long-term marriage that didn't have an exciting meet-cute to launch a fairy-tale ending. To her credit, she still tried.

"How was the chemistry between the two of you at the beginning of your relationship?" She reworded the question for my benefit.

The thing was, unlike couples who courted each other before tying the knot, there had been no gradual (or sudden) tapering of the initial spike of endorphins expected in romantic relationships in our case. In fact, the slow buildup of camaraderie and trust that happens with the constant presence and support of a reliable person in your life who is vested in your well-being had not happened.

Our arranged marriage had followed a checklist approach. The focus was on long-term compatibility, not instant infatuation. Chemistry was not part of the equation. Period. Sparks, if any, would come later. And when they arrived for us, the sparks were not the good kind.

Reluctant to explain or get defensive, I mumbled an incoherent answer. Not surprisingly, Linda's interest in my situation diminished drastically after that first session.

I knew there wasn't much for me in that group. Yet I still attended subsequent sessions purely for academic interest. I was curious about the status of the American marriage, or at least the segment represented in this group.

Every Wednesday evening, I sat in that circle, considering it a learning exercise, an experiment in observation.

Lisa and David, both of whom worked at my workplace, although in different departments, had two kids under the age of twelve. They were in their early forties and on the surface seemed pretty well-matched in terms of their careers and life goals. Lisa resented David's lack of involvement in their day-to-day lives, which left her with most of the household responsibilities, which sounded a lot like my story.

Ashley and John, the other couple in the group, disagreed about their finances. John spent his money on sports and exercise equipment, high-end clothing, and expensive gadgets, but Ashley expected John to save for their future. I was familiar with this dynamic as well.

The other women brought up their issues—divergent goals, lack of affection or concern for their well-being, among others.

I shared much in common with the women in that group. Regardless of the way in which each of us had entered matrimony, the challenges of making it work lay on the other side of the picture-perfect happily-ever-after that was often painted by children's books and glossy magazine photographs of exotic destination weddings.

The human side of us was responsible for our current state of unhappiness as a married couple. But our human side was also enmeshed within the fabric of our cultural heritage. For me, the decision to follow through or break from the marital bond was not simply a matter of individual choice. It influenced our social standing within our community and among people whose opinions we valued.

Was it possible for me to find someone to help sort out my thoughts? Could I find a counselor in the United States who was capable of addressing my issues through his or her understanding of the human nature that unites us, even in our dysfunction, without harping on the obvious cultural differences?

Could anyone address my marital troubles, which lay not only in the intrinsic differences in our individual personalities but also in the isolation we faced as a couple in the environment in which we were living?

Like a plant transplanted away from its original soil, the two of us were suffering. To relatives in India, our life in the United States seemed to be a bed of roses: we both had jobs, drove our own cars, had enrolled our child in a private preschool, and had recently been on a holiday to Maui.

We had abundant light and water, yet we lacked the nourishment that was buried in the grains of the familiar milieu of our growing-up years in India.

Had our families been around, perhaps they could have guided us when we first began to drift, but they were too far away to see the small but perceptible shift.

Perhaps we could have spoken to a wise elder who cared about us equally and provided us actionable advice to build a bridge as soon as the rift appeared, but we didn't know anyone who could step into that role.

Perhaps we could have unburdened ourselves to a qualified therapist well-versed in the cultural nuances of our story, but we had not found that person. Plus, therapy was often seen as a sign of failure and, therefore, was a last resort.

At the end of the six-week session, I was exactly where I had been the day I spotted the flyer, hope fluttering in my chest. I was still thinking of divorce and was no wiser about whether it was the right decision for me.

I ran into Lisa a few months later at the office cafeteria. We smiled awkwardly at each other, recalling the strange setting of our first meeting.

"Hello," I said.

"Hi. We finally get to meet here," Lisa said, acknowledging our common workplace even though our initial introduction had been at the divorce workshop.

"How are you?" We both asked each other the same question at the same time and stopped awkwardly.

"Did you decide to go ahead with your divorce?" Lisa asked.

"No. I'm still not sure," I said. "And you?" I asked.

"I didn't have to decide. David died in an accident three months ago. His bicycle was hit by a car, just outside our campus," she said.

Lisa's face was calm as she spoke, but I was shocked and unable to hide it. I had read about the accident in the local paper and in the office-wide email, but I had not connected the incident with someone I knew.

"I'm so sorry," I said, instinctively reaching for her hand.

"It's okay. I'm trying to get things sorted out. It's a mess, financially and otherwise. The children are upset," she replied matter-of-factly.

I didn't know what to say. I held her hand silently for a few minutes.

"Take care," I said, as we made excuses and parted.

In the days that followed, I kept going back to my conversation with Lisa and to the sessions in Linda's office where Lisa and David had passionately defended their actions, refusing to acknowledge any lack on their part to make their marriage work. They arrived together, were always polite, and on the surface seemed to be well-suited for each other. But they were unhappy.

Was unhappiness grounds for divorce? Like me, they had been unsure about spending the rest of their lives together. But would they have wanted the other to be gone forever?

Death had taken away their choice. Was Lisa's life made easier or harder by David's death?

I could not ask. I would never know.

All I knew for certain was that despite my hesitation about divorce, I was simply postponing the inevitable.

I

FALLING

Leaving

Life shrinks or expands in proportion to one's courage
~ Anais Nin

It is not often that I relive the memory of the day I left my husband's house, but when I do, I do it as a grand cinematic flashback.

From an overhead vantage point, the camera zooms in on a woman stepping down the stairs of a two-story house with a suitcase in one hand. Her face is unmoving, her jaw hard, her steps firm. With her free hand, she opens the creaky gate and walks toward a pale blue car. Even though she is aware of three pairs of eyes watching her, she doesn't look back. Her gaze is resolutely focused on the unknown future that needs all her attention.

The scene seems to be straight out of a low-budget Bollywood movie, or maybe a television soap opera, but something is off. There are no long speeches, no tears, no somber music. Just a silent exit. Perhaps it is a breaking news clip. At any moment, a reporter could step out of the shadows, push a microphone into the woman's face and let forth a barrage of questions:

How do you feel about leaving your family home?
What are you thinking right now?
Will you file for divorce?
What will happen to your child?
Your parents are not here and you don't have any close relatives in this city—where will you go?
You have never lived alone; how will you survive?
What will people say?

The questions would not be unreasonable. The woman, however, is speechless. Not because she has not given any thought to her decision; in fact, it is all she has thought about in the months and years leading to this unraveling. But this is not the time to answer questions.

She needs to get away from this toxic marriage, this claustrophobic house. She needs to take long, deep breaths. But first, she needs to save herself.

When the camera gets so close to her that she can't see anything else, the woman wonders, "How did I get to this point?"

Facing my fears

You must do the thing you think you cannot do
~ Eleanor Roosevelt

Leaving my husband's home on our sixteenth wedding anniversary meant I was homeless on my birthday.

On my first birthday as a married woman, four days after the wedding, I turned twenty-two. There was a reception in Hyderabad that evening, and without much experience or help, I had draped a rich *kanjeevaram* silk saree with a maroon and gold border over my body, twisted my long braid into a bun on my head, and stuck a larger-than-normal red bindi on my forehead.

I applied *kajal* to my eyes, the only makeup I was familiar with, slipped glass bangles onto hands dark red with henna, and adjusted the pleats of my saree.

My parents and brothers had chosen to skip the reception in Hyderabad in order to prepare for the next one in Mumbai. I stayed silent in the car ride to the venue, and despite the excitement of my birthday and the chance to meet my husband's circle of family and friends, I felt abandoned. Alone.

Arranged marriages were like this. You move from your father's home to your husband's house, trusting that the system has your back. Like the net that trapeze artists don't see but know will catch them if they fall, the tradition and the community that endorses this practice is supposed to be the invisible net that supports every couple embarking on such a marriage purely based on their faith in their family's good intentions.

Yet, the wedding celebrations were meant to be large gatherings where both families actively mingled and displayed their solidarity to the cause of the happiness of the newlywed couple.

Without the safe armor of my parents' presence amid all these strangers, I felt vulnerable and unprepared for what lay ahead. Was it a portent of things to come? A sign that I would have to do many things by myself in the future?

From my parents' point of view, everything had come together smoothly and quickly. They were unable to financially support my wish to study abroad. Notwithstanding my stellar academic record and the possibility of me securing admission and scholarship at an American university, my mother's preferred channel to enable access to the foreign education of my dreams was marriage.

Instead of sending me off alone to struggle as a graduate student on a small stipend in a new country, she figured marriage would make my path easier. My father was happy to see me "settled."

By performing *kanyadaan*, the symbolic offering of the responsibility of a daughter to the son-in-law, he had done the right thing. Marriage was the stone (millstone?) that had truly killed many birds.

Just the year before, I had pushed back on suggestions of an early marriage by insisting on getting a master's degree before embarking on such a major life change. I wasn't against marriage, just the timing of it.

"You can get married first. Then study. Your husband-to-be has agreed to it, right?"

They were right. My sole objection that marriage would be an obstruction to my plans for higher education was cast aside. I really had no case. I would have liked to be in this situation a few years down the road, preferably with a master's degree in my hand, but life doesn't always oblige by lining up events in the desired sequence. In the end, they didn't force me to marry—I could have said no.

Despite my youthful naivete, I knew life was unpredictable. I presumed life in the United States would be easier with a spouse who knew the ropes and was committed to being by my side. I was pragmatic, just like my parents, and agreed to the marriage.

A large group of extended family members from each side had arrived at the hastily arranged wedding venue in Tirupati, a temple town far away from the bustling city of Mumbai where I had grown up. But when the plans for a reception in Hyderabad hosted by my in-laws was announced, my parents asked me if I absolutely wanted them to be present.

They needed time to arrange the second reception in Mumbai for their friends who had been unable to attend the wedding. Knowing how stressful the past few weeks had been, I agreed to face the Hyderabad reception alone, knowing that I would meet my parents in Mumbai soon.

Yet, on the day of the reception, I felt like a soldier sent to battle without any training or orientation, into an alien—if not hostile—environment.

Until then, I had grown up in the shelter of my loving family in a small apartment in Mumbai. I had never lived in a hostel or spent long periods of time away from home.

Although I had traveled by train and plane to Delhi, to Bangalore, on college trips, or to visit friends or relatives, the people who received me at those destinations were familiar to me, connected by bonds of blood or affection. However, this new family (which was now mine) and their complicated inner relationships were unknown to me.

Was I being brave or naive or foolishly optimistic by agreeing to face the reception without family support? What were my parents thinking? Perhaps they trusted me more than I trusted myself.

The car that would take us to the reception venue was decorated with flowers. When my new husband, handsome in his suit and tie, got into the car beside me, I tamped down the small pinch of doubt with a smile, knowing that I had to get through the evening first, shaking hands, receiving gifts, and smiling at strangers.

I decided to look upon the event as an unusual and memorable public celebration of my birthday. I was the lucky one who got to have it all: an arranged marriage with a perfect stranger and a life in the United States and all that it promised.

The evening was nothing spectacular, but the date of the wedding did turn out to be "memorable." I could not have known then that the date that marked our union would also mark our uncoupling. It would be the date I would move out of our home, and later also be the date we would file for divorce.

It would take many more years for me to dissociate my birthday from this day of great significance and learn to joyfully celebrate my birth without linking it to my failed marriage.

On my thirty-eighth birthday, sixteen years later, I was homeless in Hyderabad.

My life was in shambles.

Yet I had much to be thankful for.

First and foremost, I was safe. My child, Shreya, was also safe.

I had a job.

A colleague I met at work, Radha, had become a good friend. Hearing of my deteriorating home situation, she had extended an invitation to move in with her if I ever felt the need to leave. When we showed up at her doorstep that morning, Radha welcomed us warmly and invited us to stay as long as we needed to. Shreya and I occupied the guest bedroom for the weekend, and on Monday, Radha and I left for work together.

I wanted my parents to help me negotiate this new turn in my life, but they were in the United States to help my younger brother and his wife, who were expecting their second child. My parents were worried and helpless, knowing that it would be a few months before they returned. After a series of frantic international phone calls, my elder brother flew in from Kolkata on the day I left my husband's house.

Although distressed by the unfolding situation, my parents were not entirely surprised by it. On their periodic visits to the United States, Amma and Dada had witnessed the strained atmosphere in my home. While Amma acknowledged my troubles, she chose to keep our discussions superficial and simple, playing with Shreya and enjoying the change of scene.

When my husband expressed interest in returning to India after spending fourteen years in the United States, I was not too keen.

My professional life was blooming, and with Shreya in kindergarten, parenting was getting easier. But our dynamic as a couple was getting worse. By moving to India, I hoped that family intervention would ease our marital situation.

Instead of yielding the desired result, my plan backfired spectacularly. Amma and Dada had probably foreseen this denouement when I had first broached the subject of returning to India. Rather than being happy to hear of my plan to return to India, they had tried to gently dissuade me.

While they might have predicted the tough road ahead, they had misjudged the speed with which things would go downhill for me after our arrival in India. Within two years of our return, I had been forced to take the unforeseen step of leaving my home, fearful for my personal safety.

Many months later, Amma would confess that the day I had left my husband's home, I had publicly declared that the rift in my marriage had gone from a small tear to a clean break, one that would be impossible to repair.

That first weekend at Radha's house, I was able to exhale and inhale deeply. I filled my lungs with fresh air and slowed my breaths, training my racing brain to gradually detach from the state of flight or fright in which it had existed for the past few months. I was simultaneously energized and paralyzed by all that I needed to do.

In a city where I had no personal network to tap into, and with no knowledge of organizations that assisted in such situations, I had to figure things out myself.

At quiet moments, feelings of abandonment from the day of my wedding reception resurfaced. I pushed them down. Just as I had done all those years ago, I needed to set aside the "why me" and focus on the "what next."

On my birthday, my brother picked up Shreya from school, and after I returned from work, we went for a boat ride on Hussain Sagar Lake. The giant Buddha statue watched us benevolently as we ate *chana bhatura* at the food court at sunset.

Shreya handed me a birthday card with a shy smile, her eight-year-old face scrunched up with anticipation.

"Happy Birthday, Amma. I will always be with you."

Her childish scrawl and her innocent words were exactly what I needed to hear.

Too moved to cry, I hugged her close, unsure of what lay ahead for the two of us. But we had each other. Her small hand made mine feel strong. Her words gave me a reason to pull myself together.

I had to do it. I had no choice.

That first choice to leave an unhappy home had put me on a path strewn with more choices. Such was life.

I had to accept it without looking for certainties.

Making a list

~~

Nothing in life is to be feared, it is only to be understood
~ Marie Curie

I sat alone in a dark room, gazing at the row of lamps that illuminated the path from the gate to the entrance of the neighbor's house. I could hear shouts and murmurs as children lit firecrackers and ran away, amused and scared. A dazzling light and sound show preceded the dense fog that enveloped everything with a thick chemical odor.

The families were dressed, I was sure, in colorful, festive clothes: the women resplendent in heavy silk sarees, the men and kids fussing in traditional attire. My oft-washed, soft cotton outfit was faded, but its comfortable texture was familiar, unlike the chair by the window in which I mulled over this unusual Diwali.

Ten days ago, I had left my husband's house and moved into Radha's home. Sixteen years is a long time, but I had made the decision to leave after much deliberation. I knew I had done the right thing because I could finally breathe.

Perhaps this is what people call the calm after the storm. The stuff of nightmares had come to pass and I was still alive. Now it was time to figure out the next steps.

I had a job but no training for the life that lay ahead. At the age of twenty-two, I had been an eager bride, expecting a Bollywood version of my very own "happily-ever-after" story to play out in the United States.

But nothing had prepared me for this detour.

There was so much to do: find a place to live, figure out school arrangements, manage my finances, be a single parent. Was I willing to do it alone? Could I?

Bursts of happy laughter interrupted my thoughts. Families come together for festivals; they do not disintegrate like mine had.

Shreya was at her father's place for the holiday. I had seen no reason for her to share my anxiety about the future, at least not today. She was six when we had arrived in India two years ago and she'd settled easily in school. She enjoyed festivals because she loved wearing colorful clothes and was particularly fearless in lighting crackers for Diwali, the festival of lights.

I knew she would be having a good time at her father's house, although her excitement was muted this time—though not because of our split home situation but because she was worried about the new puppy that had been added to the household a month before our departure. Dogs hated this noisy festival and now I did too.

My brother had returned to his home in Kolkata and Radha had gone to her parents' place for Diwali. She had asked us to come along, but I had politely refused. I desperately needed to get my act together.

Never had I imagined that there would be a Diwali celebration in my future where I would be sitting alone on an evening when people gathered to eat, laugh, and celebrate. For the first time in days, I let myself cry.

Tears don't come easily to me. Was it because I was born between two boys and hated being teased—"you cry like a girl!"—each time we had a squabble? Or was it because of Amma, who never cried? Amma believed that tears solved nothing. Perhaps it gave a physical release, but it changed neither the situation nor its outcome.

Yet I cried for hours. There was no one watching me or stopping me. Like an injured animal left to fend for itself in an unfriendly landscape, I wailed. Scenes of the past played like a movie clip in my mind. I saw myself as the young bride with stars in her eyes, the girl with a wide smile who had stepped joyfully into the adventure of her fairy-tale life, expecting only one shade of happiness.

I wept for the loss of my innocence, for the erosion of my faith in marriage, for the uncertainty of a future that depended solely on me.

My life ahead would now be strewn with the bumps that I might have encountered earlier had I taken a different path.

I might have struggled as an impoverished student in the United States if I had insisted on pursuing my higher education alone as many of my peers had done. But I had taken the shortcut of marriage that my parents had offered and now I had to face a long detour that would nullify all the notional gains of that decision. I would have to face the very hardships that my parents had sought to shield me from.

I could not sleep. I did not feel like eating. Being alone was a blessing in some ways. There was no one to inquire about my mood or fuss over my lack of appetite.

Had I ever felt this hopeless? This lost? This lonely? Yes.

Eleven years ago, I had felt the same way.

Dejected. Disoriented. Depressed.

The joy of graduating with a PhD from a prestigious university in the United States had not tempered the sharp pain I felt each time I thought about my miscarriage. Tears would spring up unannounced—at the sight of a baby in a stroller, in front of the display window at a maternity boutique, or at Toys "R" Us. The inability to carry a pregnancy to term, the diagnosis of infertility, and the magnitude of failure at not being able to do something so simple that almost everyone else could do had paralyzed me.

I lost weight. I lost my sense of purpose. I felt worthless.

Yet one day, things changed, but not because I got pregnant. I didn't.

As I drove along a familiar street, a random thought took root: "If I cannot be a mother, what CAN I be? There must be a purpose to my life. I don't know what it is, but I must find out."

A sense of calm came over me. I decided to do something every day, however mundane, to regain a foothold in the life I already had, despite the baby-sized hole in it.

All I needed to do was focus on each day. Take baby steps.

I bought a cookbook. I signed up for a singing class. I called up an old friend. And it worked.

Drop by nourishing drop, a deep ocean of serenity filled up inside me. And as I sat in Radha's house, I knew that I needed to do the same thing again.

On the moonless Diwali night, a spray of flower-shaped light illuminated the room. I stood up to watch the children laughing and chasing each other with glowing sparklers.

I had yearned for a child, not knowing if I would ever experience motherhood. It had taken time, but my daughter's birth had brightened my life. Her arrival had brought chaos as well as joy.

And here I was, once again wondering if life would ever be the same.

Deep down, I knew the answer: No, it wouldn't.

But there was a grand plan beyond my understanding that had brought me here.

I had taken a walk down the road of depression once, devaluing the education that I had worked hard to acquire, wallowing in the misery of being childless.

Now I had a child to love. She needed me to be a reliable parent. I could not allow myself to collapse into a puddle.

Like Tom Hanks in *Sleepless in Seattle*, I needed to take one step at a time. "Get out of bed. Breathe in and out. Until I don't have to remind myself to do it."

So, I made a list: inquire about apartment rentals, check the balance in my bank account, and inform the school.

Every step would take me closer to the new way of living, and soon it would become second nature to me.

It was customary to embark on a new project by taking a bite of something sweet. The box of Diwali sweets from my office was within reach, so I took one sweet bite to mark the festival and another to mark the beginning of the rest of my life.

Asking for a hug

Paradise is attained by touch ~ Helen Keller

The first thing on my list seemed to be the hardest: finding a place to rent.

Did I need an agent? Should I look at the classifieds in the newspaper? In the era before apps and Google, the practicalities of life could be overwhelming if you didn't know where to begin.

The agents listed in the newspaper sounded unprofessional and sleazy, high on eagerness but low on details. Every interaction left me with a mildly nauseated feeling.

I decided to start from the inside out and begin with the people I knew. Without divulging details, I asked two of my closest colleagues about apartment rentals. When one suggested a house (not an apartment) in a leafy neighborhood not far from our office, I made an appointment to see the place the following weekend.

Choosing a place to live with Shreya would be the first time I would make such a decision in my life, and I couldn't figure out how to evaluate the options.

Should I find something close to Shreya's school? Or close to my work? Should I choose a location where friends could provide support if needed, even if it was farther away from either work or school? Or should I focus solely on minimizing my expenses, beginning with rent?

Comfort, convenience, and cost—optimizing all three seemed impossible.

The four-bedroom duplex house was bigger than what I needed, but it was within my budget and close to my workplace located on the outskirts of the city.

"Who all will be staying in the house, madam?"

The prospective landlord, a seedy-looking man with curly black hair asked me with a creepy smile. He had quickly concealed his look of surprise at seeing me arrive alone but had not asked for details. I looked like a stern schoolteacher in my modest cotton saree and my hair held back with a clip. I tried to put on an air of nonchalance, trying to cover up the fact that this was my first time renting a home on my own.

"My daughter and I," I replied.

I saw his brain ticking. Would my business card, printed with the logo of a reputed company and my name with the prefix of "Dr." overpower his doubts about my irregular situation? His home had been vacant since a burglary a few months ago, and despite our mutual apprehensions, we were both in a fix.

I had to first decide my home location and then make a list of appliances, furniture, and other items required to get a functioning home ready as soon as possible.

Money was low. So was my self-confidence.

Was it fair that I had to go through all this alone?

I didn't want to call my parents and burden them with unnecessary details. Just as they kept their minor illnesses hidden from me during the years I had lived abroad, I wanted to spare them these minute details.

Radha had been my rock, keeping Shreya busy along with her kids on weeknights after we returned home from work.

"How was house hunting?" she asked when I returned. Since Shreya was with her father on weekends, I tried to pack in as many things as I could, giving myself no time to wallow in self-pity.

"I think I have found the place. The landlord is a bit creepy, but the rent is reasonable and it's close to the office. But the house is huge and farther away from Shreya's school. I'm not sure whether that's the right thing to do," I said.

"Shreya will have a longer ride on the school bus, that's all. You need to make sure you have more time to manage everything," Radha said.

She was right. I needed to prioritize myself, something I had stopped doing long ago. Even as one half of a married couple, I had taken on more than my fair share of responsibilities, often treating my comfort as "optional." The difference now was that I didn't have the support or security of a spouse. I was truly on my own. I had to think differently about my life, my health, and also my comfort.

"Thanks, Radha," I said, glad to have her wise counsel. She smiled and nodded.

I made up my mind to call the landlord the next day to confirm.

"Do you need anything else?" she asked, as we cleared up after dinner.

"Yes. A hug," I said after a long pause.

She immediately walked over and put her arms around me in a tight embrace. I rested my head on her shoulder, tears collecting at the corners of my eyes. She couldn't see them, but she could sense my vulnerability.

"You are doing great. You know that you can stay with us for as long as you want. There is no hurry. Our girls enjoy being together, and we can continue going to the office as we are doing now."

I nodded silently. I needed her words. I needed her touch. But I also needed to get back on my feet.

People hesitate to ask for money when they need it, but money exchange is just a cold transaction between people, one that can be given and taken back. Touch, on the other hand, is a warm offering of generosity whose value lies in knowing that it can never be returned, at least not in the same way.

Asking my friend for a hug was a courageous act.

As I soaked in her goodwill and strength, I felt a sense of healing, as if a piece of my DNA was repairing itself.

Later I would remember this moment as not only the nadir of my despair but also the moment I understood the healing power of touch.

In the years that followed, I would silently hug students, friends, and colleagues going through a rough patch. Once words are exhausted, a loving touch can do much more to show solidarity, concern, and support.

There are many things I have been sorry for in my life, many mistakes and misunderstandings caused by my words and actions that I find difficult to defend in retrospect. But I am proud of having asked for a hug, uncaring of whether I would be viewed as soft or incompetent.

By asking, I learned an important lesson: expressing vulnerability makes us stronger.

Money matters

Money won't create success, the freedom to make it will
~ Nelson Mandela

Money, they say, makes the world go around. I would soon learn the truth behind this adage.

Except for the first six months of my life in the United States, I worked for the entire duration of my marriage. Given our frugal life—rented apartments, second-hand cars, bargain shopping—we should have had a reasonable corpus of savings. And perhaps we did, but I didn't have access to it.

Like most women of my generation, I had trusted my husband. My salary was paid into our joint account, which we used to manage our respective portions of the household. I took care of groceries, Shreya's day care/preschool fees, clothes, etc. He paid the rent and utility bills and was supposed to manage our money, including investments. I had my credit card, knowledge of how much I made, and one basic rule: never spend more than you earn.

On a daily basis, I did not worry about how much money we had in our bank account. I knew that some of our savings had been used to build our house in Hyderabad the year of Shreya's birth.

However, when we returned to India, we spent some more on upgrading the kitchen and bathrooms to meet our expectations as returned ex-pats. What had happened to the rest of the money in our US accounts? For all my bookish smarts, there was much about money (and relationships) that I had yet to learn.

Like an unfortunate heroine in a Bollywood film, I had left the house in distress with a suitcase, fearing for my life and sanity. Money had not been at the forefront of my concerns. After all, I had a job that paid a decent salary each month.

Dada had helped me open my first bank account in Mumbai with the first scholarship money I had received in grade 6. It had been shored up in the following years with other checks received while I was in college, cash gifts from relatives, and savings from the monthly pocket money that Dada handed out. I had closed that account when I left Mumbai after the wedding.

Upon my return, when I accepted my current job offer, my employer had facilitated the opening of a new salary account at a local bank. It was my first solo account as an adult in India, one that received an influx of funds at the end of every month.

To my pleasant surprise, I had found the salary increments and bonuses in India to be more generous than those I had received in the United States. When I was given stock options for my excellent performance, I had even been pushed to open a trading account in order to receive the stock grant.

In two years, I had saved a decent amount of money. More importantly, it was money that was under my sole, direct control.

In theory, I should have been in a comfortable position to pay the deposit for the rental, but in reality, I did not have any money in my bank account thanks to one misstep.

Months before the deteriorating home situation became unbearable, I had begun thinking about moving out. It was clear that life with in-laws in such close proximity was destroying the tenuous relationship that had endured in the United States.

"Why don't we invest in a flat near Hitech City?" I asked my husband one day.

"We already own this house. Why do we need another one in the same city?"

Clearly, we thought differently on this topic, just like we disagreed on most others. Having another place made sense to me. Even if we didn't live there, it could be a source of rental income down the line or it could just be a sanctuary that I could furnish to my taste and escape to when I needed a break. The mere thought of having such a place made me happy, and I was convinced about the merit of my idea.

Not inclined to buy jewelry or splurge on branded fashion, a part of me wanted to expand my investment portfolio, even though this was another topic that we didn't speak about.

I inquired about reputed builders and the possibility of getting a bank loan to fund my home-buying project. Finally, I found something that looked promising: a well-known builder was launching the second phase of an existing project in a good location.

It was close to a well-respected school and in the proximity of burgeoning office spaces for the tech industry that was converting Hyderabad into a much sought-after destination.

I wrote a sizable check for an 1,800-square-foot apartment that the builder promised would be ready in two years. It wiped out all the money in my account. Two weeks later, I was homeless.

When I moved into Radha's house, I did not have enough money to pay the deposit on the house that I needed to rent.

How had I, a smart, sensible, bold girl (as I thought of myself), come to be in this situation? I had held a series of jobs that had paid me reasonably well. Beginning with a decent student stipend as a PhD student, then as a postdoctoral fellow, and later as a research scientist at a multinational pharmaceutical company, I had worked through my infertility phase and in the early years of Shreya's life, despite being racked with working mother guilt.

What had all of those struggles and sacrifices added up to? I should have been financially secure for the rainy day that had arrived, but I had nothing.

The only ray of hope was the knowledge that my salary would be credited to my account in a few days. But what until then? Should I borrow money? If so, from whom? My parents were in the United States and could not access their India accounts.

My brothers? It didn't feel right to ask them to rescue me. Friends? I was already indebted to the people who were helping me in so many ways, I could not impose on them any further.

Never in my life had I felt so poor. I was financially and emotionally bankrupt. I logged into my bank account, hoping for some miracle, but nothing had changed since I had last checked. The numbers confirmed what I already knew: life had hit rock bottom.

I called the landlord to confirm my decision to rent but requested him to wait until the end of the month for the deposit. He agreed.

When the salary came in, I had a pleasant surprise. Certain long overdue reimbursements, including a big chunk for the medical claim for my mother's cataract surgery, had been paid up. A least expected but most welcome ray of sunshine!

Money did make the world go around.

II

STARTING OVER

Coming home

*It isn't for the moment you are struck that you need courage,
but for that long uphill climb back to sanity and
faith and security ~ Anne Morrow Lindbergh*

My new home was huge. A tiny metal gate opened into a small courtyard that led to the front door. A spacious living and dining area occupied most of the space downstairs. Two bedrooms were located at the back, with a bathroom in between, and the kitchen was off to the side. The upper floor had two larger bedrooms, a bathroom, and a door leading to an L-shaped terrace. One of the downstairs bedrooms and the kitchen had doors that led outside.

When I told my boss that I needed flexibility in the coming weeks, he thankfully didn't ask too many questions. Perhaps the office grapevine had provided him some background. Surprisingly, help with logistics, not a trivial thing in India, came in many forms, including information on how to apply for a phone connection and a gas cylinder.

The landlord left behind a few pieces of furniture, including a sofa and a bed in the smallest bedroom. When Shreya and I moved in with our suitcases, our voices echoed off the stone walls in the cavernous rooms.

"Helloooooo. Helllllooooo," Shreya would yell into the empty house, unafraid.

I bought necessary appliances—a fridge, a toaster, and a pressure cooker. I needed a functional house before anything else. The smaller details of curtains and cushions that could turn the huge, impersonal house into a home could wait.

The neighborhood was green, and our street was remarkably quiet and isolated from the traffic and noise of the Mumbai highway that was located just a few hundred meters away.

Shreya's presence bolstered my resolve to set myself straight, but when she asked to visit her father (and the puppy) on the weekend, I did not refuse. She skipped off happily without asking too many questions.

Children have a remarkable ability to focus only on the good, and Shreya was no exception.

On my first weekend alone in the big house, I finished dinner early and tried to relax with a book.

Was the terrace door closed? Yes. The kitchen door? Closed. The back bedroom door leading to the outside was permanently locked, a precondition to my move, to which the landlord had agreed. That left the front door and the outside grill door. Both were shut.

Through the curtainless windows, I saw the flicker of a television screen and heard faint laughter from the house directly opposite mine. As a car turned into our street, the arc of its headlights briefly lit up the walls. The engine turned off. Doors opened and closed. The sounds tapered off before stopping completely.

The streetlight outside my window illuminated the bare spaces of my new home, a reflection of the emptiness in my heart.

I locked myself inside the bedroom, hoping to come out only after daybreak. I was thirsty but couldn't bring myself to open the door and walk to the kitchen. I needed to use the bathroom, but even that required opening the bedroom door, the only barrier between me and the rest of the spooky house. I turned over on my other side and plumped the pillow.

I chanted Sanskrit *shlokas*, prayers that I had learned as a child, to ward off nightmares. I tried counting sheep. The phone marked the time as 1 a.m. and my thirst intensified along with the urge to pee. The night was a mountain of discomfort that I scaled only when the first rays of the sun streamed in through the window. I welcomed the morning with a dash to the bathroom.

Saturday stretched interminably. Perhaps I should have opted for a small apartment and not this large house. I was a city girl, having grown up in a tiny apartment surrounded by family members, one of whom was always at home. The only time I had been forced to sleep alone in Mumbai was a year before my wedding.

I had returned from a college trip to Chennai and found my house locked. A helpful neighbor had given me the key with a letter informing me that the family had taken off on an impromptu pilgrimage.

I had managed during the day but could not bring myself to sleep alone in the empty flat at night. Tejal, my childhood best friend and neighbor, had come to my rescue by agreeing to spend the night with me. A light sleeper and an alert one, she was the last to fall asleep and first to wake up when the milkman rang the bell at 6 a.m.

I shuddered at the memory of that night from years ago. Had I not learned anything in the intervening years? I had crisscrossed continents, qualified as a scientist, become a mother, and yet here I was, terrified of spending a night alone.

In the United States, there had been a handful of days when I had stayed by myself in our apartment, first in Maryland and later in California, when his job had required him to travel, although it wasn't a frequent occurrence. I had myself traveled and stayed alone in hotel rooms, initially as a student when I attended scientific conferences and later when my job demanded it. Yet, this was different.

Being alone for a short time versus choosing to be alone for the foreseeable future were not the same. If I was having so much trouble on the first weekend, what would happen to me in the long run?

Had I been too hasty in leaving?

I had not left after one huge fight or misunderstanding. I had made the decision after much deliberation. In the two years since our return to Hyderabad, the tension had slowly escalated. Was the stress of adjusting back to life in India after many years in the United States to blame? Was it the close presence of in-laws that had made our inherently volatile relationship flare up? Or was it our basic incompatibility that had reached unmanageable levels?

All I knew was that in the past few months, I had felt shut out, badgered, and cornered; I'd been yelled at, blamed for everything that was not going well, and repeatedly asked to leave the home. On the last day, I had feared for my life.

Had I been hasty in leaving?

The answer came back surprisingly strong and unambiguous: NO!

Even though I was anxious, especially at night, I was finally breathing more easily and freely.

No matter how difficult, choosing freedom over toxic familiarity would always be the correct choice.

Requesting help

Before you know kindness, you must lose things
~ Naomi Shihab Nye

When our family unit of three broke down to the smallest possible structure of one parent and one child, I had to figure things out. Quickly. No matter how dysfunctional, we had been two adults and one child. I was no longer on one side of a seesaw trying to keep the balance on my end. I had to run to the middle and keep hopping to hold both sides steady while juggling major decisions and minor chores.

Growth spurts, it turned out, were not just for young children. Moving out gave me the impetus to grow up and be truly independent.

When I put in a request for a landline telephone connection, the company insisted on knowing the phone number of a neighbor before assigning one to me. I walked over to the house with which I shared a common wall. Hearing the creaky gate, a woman named Kiran stepped out.

I felt an instant camaraderie with the smiling, striking woman with short grey hair. Her serious-looking glasses contrasted with her bright smile. Within a few minutes, I found out that Kiran was also from Mumbai. She lived with her widowed mother and two sons, a fact that felt reassuring. She responded generously to my request.

My new house was close to my workplace. It saved me an hour of commute time each day, but, as suspected, added to Shreya's bus ride to school. When I called the school to change the bus route, it became clear that Shreya would have to leave home much earlier and make new friends on the school bus and in the new neighborhood.

Before the split, Shreya and I would ride together in the car on school days, a daily ritual that we both enjoyed. Raju, our driver, cleaned the car each morning and would take us first to Shreya's school and then to my office. Shreya returned home by school bus in the afternoon. All this had to change.

I had no choice in this matter. By making one decision to separate from her father, I had picked a course that would force me to make many other choices every single day to make our life work and to ensure Shreya's wellbeing.

School hours and office hours do not ever match. I learned that in the United States. In India, however, there was no concept of after-school day care or work-life balance. My job involved interactions with collaborators in the United States, which required late evening telecons that had to be attended from the office.

Even on days without calls, Shreya's school bus arrived at 4 p.m. This had not been a problem earlier because her father or grandparents had been home. Now, she would have to enter an empty house, alone.

Unable to figure out where to begin, I walked over to the house across our narrow street and stood at the gate. A lady with a long braid approached with a smile.

"Hello. My name is Ranjani. I have just moved into number 303," I said, pointing to my door where Shreya stood, with her school uniform and backpack.

"I am Kumari. Nice to meet you." Kumari smiled at Shreya.

"I wanted to ask you if you can help me find a maid. I need someone to come at 4 p.m. and pick my daughter up from the bus stop. She can do the cleaning and mopping and wait until I get back, usually by 6 p.m."

Unlike me, Shreya was not afraid to be alone. But she was only eight years old. When she arrived home tired and hungry, she needed supervision and a snack.

Kumari offered to spread the word. The next morning, Tirupattama, a skinny woman with a silly grin knocked on the door. She didn't mind the odd timings that I proposed. Even though the house had nothing of much value, I was reluctant to give her a key.

I opted to let Shreya keep the key in her backpack. After Tirupattama picked her up at the bus stop, Shreya would open the door and Tirupattama would do her work. Shreya was intimidated by the woman's big white teeth with large gaps that showed when she smiled, but I had no choice but to agree despite my misgivings.

Most days I tried to come home early, not just for Shreya but also for Raju, the driver, whose life had been upset by my sudden move. He lived within walking distance of the old neighborhood, which was nowhere close to my new home.

"I cannot come here by 8 o'clock, Madam. I have to leave home very early and change two buses," Raju said.

He didn't explicitly put into words another of my fears: that he wanted to quit. The car and a portion of Raju's salary was covered by my compensation package at work. The day I had signed the employment contract, I had not realized how much of a boon it would prove to be. In the weeks since my move, Raju's support had been invaluable. I might have left that house with just a suitcase, but it had been ferried in a car that bore my name (or the name of my employer). And now I was at risk of losing that too.

The truth was, I was not just afraid to be alone—I was unprepared. Even though I considered myself to be a free-thinking, independent individual, the strands of my life had always been enmeshed with others, something that was now being revealed to me in so many ways.

Breaking one bond was not the end; it was the beginning. It wasn't a thread that had snapped. The entire net of relationships built on the assumption of "ever after" had collapsed. As I kept falling down an abyss, it was not my life that flashed in front of me but an enactment of all my fears.

Despite driving over 100,000 miles in the United States, I was terrified of driving in India. In the two years since my return, I had expressed no interest in getting into the driver's seat. But now was not the time for it.

If Raju left, I would lose my mobility. I offered to increase his salary and pay for his transport each day, and he agreed to stay. We both knew that this was not the last conversation we would have on this subject, but for that day, I had averted a minor disaster.

Help came in many forms. Some were offered freely, but for others, I would have to pay.

Seeking solace

Prayer is a relationship; half the job is mine
~ Elizabeth Gilbert

The campus of Apollo hospital in Jubilee Hills was always busy; a stream of cars and wailing ambulances carried the ill or injured to the entrance of the building, its corridors littered with patients and their families, weighed down by fear and heavy with hope.

Not far from where this daily drama of life and death played out was a small temple. I don't remember how I came across this hidden treasure, but one day I found it, nestled in a green corner of the hospital premises.

The first time I stepped up those polished granite steps, I had no idea that I would repeatedly return in various states of despair, or that this space would become my oasis of calm that would give me the strength to get through the next day and preserve my sanity as my life crumbled.

The city of Hyderabad is home to more than one hundred temples dedicated to Lord Venkateshwara, the popular local deity.

From the top of Naubat Pahad where he sits in marble splendor in the Birla Temple, showering blessings on tourists who gather for a stunning view of the lake, to the relatively modest premises on the outskirts at Chilkur, where he blesses the hordes of hopeful aspirants seeking a US visa (thereby acquiring the nickname of Visa Balaji), the dark and powerful Venkateshwara is uniformly revered for his generosity.

In the first two decades of my life, I had seen my share of temples on pilgrimages to many corners of India with my deeply religious family. As a child, I had disliked, and even feared, temples, especially on festival days when they were full of unruly people. In adulthood, I had chosen to keep my personal communion with God a private affair, conducted in the privacy of my home.

A simple daily ritual of lighting a lamp in front of an uncluttered altar and the silent recitation of prayers learned in childhood constituted my spiritual practice.

In the fourteen years we spent in the United States, we'd only gone a few times to visit temples. The majestic Venkateswara temple in Pittsburgh had been more than a four-hour ride from the Washington DC metropolitan area, where I had first arrived as a young bride.

The local temple, not far from our apartment in suburban Maryland, was built during the early years of our marriage, but once I started graduate school in Baltimore, and later after we moved to California, temple visits rarely landed on the top of our to-do list.

Back in India, it was impossible to miss the temples that graced every street corner. The newly inaugurated temple down the street had multiple shrines devoted to numerous gods and goddesses. It resembled a big banner movie with a large star cast. Disappointed with its lack of serenity, I stayed away.

That is, until I found this boutique temple on the hospital premises with its perfect welcoming vibe.

In the two years since moving back from the United States, I escaped to my secret temple, as I liked to call it, on days when I felt listless and hopeless. Many evenings after work, I looked for excuses to delay going back to the claustrophobic place called home. I walked around the sanctum, inhaling the mixed fragrance of ghee-soaked cotton wicks, vapors of sweet incense, and the intensity of the prayers of the devotees.

My heart slowed down as my body got accustomed to the change of pace. I would find my favorite spot by a pillar, away from other devotees, and bite into the pungent leaves of holy basil, the taste of which stayed on my tongue after swallowing the cool, flavored water, offered by the priest, from my cupped palm.

As twilight approached, a couple of bare-chested and bearded junior priests would appear, their stocky frames crowned with tight coils of hair on top of their heads. They would sit side by side and adjust the microphone. Turning off the background noise of piped devotional music, they would begin to recite the Vishnu Sahasranamam at precisely 6:30 p.m. under the stern gaze of the senior priest.

The first time I heard this chanting, I leaned against the pillar and closed my eyes, lulled by the cool breeze and the familiar sing-song tones of Sanskrit words uttered in unison. They took me back to my childhood where I had heard M. S. Subbulakshmi repeat them every morning on our much-loved cassette player.

Perhaps it was the nostalgia of a happier time of my life or the power of prayer, but I returned home feeling calm and more hopeful. In a box containing religious paraphernalia, I found a copy of Vishnu Sahasranamam printed in Devanagari script on a compact three-inch by two-inch booklet.

I put the booklet in my purse, bought a CD, and listened to the soothing chant on my way to the office.

For young boys preparing for a vocation as priest, the ability to memorize and recite Sanskrit shlokas is a skill that is imparted to them at an early age. The uncluttered mind of a child is a receptive space to plant complex words and syllables whose meaning is explained to them much later. Despite having been schooled at a Catholic institution, Amma taught me many shlokas.

Whether inside the walls of school or outside, I enjoyed reading and learning. Most of all, I liked to show off my ability to memorize. I remembered how I would loudly recite the shlokas with ease, taking great pride in perfecting the pronunciation and intonation. Just the thought of those simple childhood days made me smile.

I assigned myself the task of learning the Vishnu Sahasranamam, the one thousand names of Vishnu, as an exercise to stimulate my brain. The CD played in the car and at home while I sat with the little book in my lap, trying to get my ears to focus and my tongue to enunciate the complicated syllables.

Several times a week, I would stop at the temple in the evenings just in time to join the chanting. The exclusive focus on the Sanskrit words gave my mind a break from the dark clouds of gloom that accompanied me to work and back each day.

Was I in denial of the irreversible disintegration of my marriage? Was the temple an easy escape? Or was the chanting a fervent appeal?

Faith is a funny thing. It holds out the option of surrender when everything else has failed.

The power of prayer lies in its ability to give us permission to put down our burdens and trust that the universe will have our backs.

Even as the cynical part of me didn't expect a miracle to happen by merely adding my voice to those of the priests who chanted the entire *sahasranamam* without glancing at a written version, the trusting younger me had once been nurtured by the simple act of participation in a communal ritual.

My problems (and me) became insignificant for those forty-five minutes of the chanting cycle. In that sliver of space where everything—including past mistakes, future mishaps, and the uncertain present—was suspended, I could catch my breath and ease the pressure on my chest, even if it was only for a few minutes a day.

In my new neighborhood, far from the bustle of Apollo Hospital, I found a temple that offered a quiet space for chanting and contemplation. Located beside a narrow street filled with honking vehicles and loud chatter, the inner courtyard somehow managed to shrug off the cares of the outside world.

The stone floor was pitted and marked by the footfalls of thousands of other hopefuls who had walked here before me, each carrying their own pleas. On weekends when Shreya was away, I walked over to the temple at sunset, leaned against a pillar, and opened my book.

Although the nights were still long, I had learned to keep a bottle of water by my bed and use the toilet before locking myself in for the night. What helped most was the calm brought on by the chanting. It covered me like a soothing blanket in an empty house, casting aside the futile contemplation of an unknown future that haunted me during my waking hours.

Expressing myself

There are homes you run from, and there are homes you run to
~ Laura Cunningham

The house was big but bare. Except for a single bed in the small bedroom downstairs and a well-used sofa that the landlord left behind, the rooms echoed with our spoken words and my unspoken doubts. Built with dark grey stones that retained heat long after sunset, the rooms would heat up in the summer months, a fact that I would learn a few months later. But for now, the bare windows allowed the morning rays free access into every nook and corner of the house, illuminating its emptiness.

An empty room can be an instrument for introspection. It was a reflection of the void created by the decision to distance myself from a relationship that had defined me to others and to myself. If I was not a wife, who was I? I was removing a label that marked my place in a social system, but was I still "me" without that label?

An empty room can also be a catalyst for transformation. It was a reminder that I could now begin to shape the space around me exactly as I wanted, literally and metaphorically. By carefully choosing what I wanted to put into the space, by mindfully avoiding easy solutions, I could find myself.

Going inward was not easy. By looking outward, I could create my ideal home, a dream that I had previously deferred in the interest of family harmony.

I decided to create a home from scratch, something that would reflect my tastes and preferences with a combination of objects and energy that would add up to a safe and inviting space for the people and experiences I wanted to welcome into my life.

In the first year of our life together in suburban Maryland, my husband and I had managed with a mishmash of things that were lent, gifted, or borrowed: an L-shaped grey couch with plaid upholstery left by the previous tenant, a circular coffee table with a glass top and a square four-seater dining table. Some of these made it across the country to California and others were discarded along the way.

But I had never felt strongly enough about home furnishings to insist on specific items. Our home was an odd combination of objects and keepsakes, a hodgepodge of items that reflected the state of our marriage. Each of us added things that we liked without concern for whether it appealed to the other or fit into a cohesive greater scheme.

Although it felt strange to be setting up a house alone, I now had a chance to finally make choices that defined me and my hopes. I did not have to defer, second guess, or give in to please another person. Naturally, I was terrified. Stumped by the small stuff. It was the simple things that paralyzed me. My life had been defined by my conditioning.

To gain confidence, to put myself firmly on a path to independence, I needed to practice making small choices. I decided to begin by making this cavernous house into a cozy home.

A fridge, a cooking stove, and a washing machine were necessities. So was a bed with a comfortable mattress, and curtains. From a vendor outside Ratnadeep supermarket who sold cotton curtains on a cart, I carefully selected a few colors and sizes for the various windows for each of the downstairs rooms. I picked up cushions from Shopper Stop.

At the annual crafts fair at Shilparamam, on a whim, I bought a bright red, two-feet by three-feet rectangular mat with a golden border that looked like a resplendent saree in my favorite shade of red. It was an odd-size mat of woven cane—too small to lie down on, too big to sit on. But it caught my eye. I had no idea what to do with it, but I added it to the pile of practical bedsheets, pillowcases, and cushion covers.

When the bed and mattress arrived, I had to decide what to do about the two cotton mattresses that Radha had given us when we had left her home.

"Do you want the mattresses back?" I asked Radha when I updated her about the progress on the home front.

"Not really, they were spare ones for guests. You can keep them for now," she said.

The living room had a small sofa and two one-seater chairs, leaving a lot of empty space. I had always thought that a small mattress on the floor covered with a bright bedspread and comfortable cushions added a touch of casual warmth and lightened a formal living space into a livable one. Why not pull the cotton mattresses in the living room?

Instinctively, a space for my red mat opened up, not on the floor but on the wall against which the mattresses were lined up. I had wondered how to cover up the two ugly nails that protruded from that wall. Now I knew. The nails were at the exact distance at which I could easily tuck the edges of my gorgeous new mat. Soon, the red mat hung like a defiant flag, its gilded border softening the statement made by its bold color.

An unconventional move perhaps but certainly a statement piece that often turned into a conversation starter.

I knew I had done the right thing with the mattresses because they eventually became a welcoming space for Shreya and her new friends. They lounged on them, read books, played Uno, or concocted make-believe games. When the walls reverberated with the innocent laughter and joy that children bring to the present moment without the baggage of the past or worries about the future, a great weight lifted from my shoulders.

The bedroom was now comfortable and restful, with curtains that gave us privacy and shade, but we had no place to sit and enjoy our meals. It was time to add a dining table.

One weekend, I went to the street beside Lakdi Ka Pul, a narrow lane lined with shops that sold cane furniture. They had tables and swings, small stools, and end tables that looked attractive. Although not as elegant as the expensive furniture displayed in the well-lit showrooms that lined the wide avenues of Banjara Hills, these looked comfier.

Wood always gave a warm vibe, unlike the harsh metallic surfaces preferred in modern designs. I couldn't afford expensive teak furniture, but I did have choices within my limited budget.

I had spaced out my purchases sensibly, not wanting to splurge the entire month's salary on setting up a temporary home. Who knew how long we would stay here? Yet, I didn't want our life to feel like a prolonged wait at a transit stop on the route to a different destination. Stranded or not, this is where we were parked for now and I had to make my home a welcoming space.

I selected a small round glass-top dining table with four chairs. The wooden support for the table was sturdy, although the chairs felt a bit flimsy. But the price was right.

After a few minutes of back-and-forth conversation and good-natured bargaining, Rahim, the shopkeeper, agreed to throw in free delivery, promising to send the items before the end of the day.

Since Shreya was away, I spent the evening reading. It was getting late, and I was concerned about the dining table that had still not arrived. I was not comfortable opening my door to strangers at night. I called Rahim, who assured me that the table was on the way.

Around 8:30 p.m., I heard creaking sounds outside my gate. I cautiously peered from the windows and saw a frail man unloading the table and chairs from a hand-pulled cart. I had expected an automobile to deposit my furniture, not a human-powered cart!

I ran out to help. The man who appeared to be in his sixties wiped sweat off his face as he put the last piece inside my house.

"Water?" I asked.

"No, I am fasting for Ramzan. I will go home and break my fast with my family," he smiled, handing me the receipt.

How could this man have walked all this way, dragging my furniture, without having eaten anything all day?

I had bargained for free delivery with Rahim. And he in turn had chosen the cheapest way to fulfill my demand. I felt guilty and sad.

I asked the man to wait and went to get my wallet. I pulled out an amount equal to the price of the furniture and handed it to him.

"Go and eat with your family. Use it for Eid," I said.

He looked at me with unbelieving eyes. For a daily wage laborer, this was equal to several days of income. But it was a holy month for him. It didn't seem right that he had to perform hard physical work while fasting in order to support his family. The money would not change his life, but it would ease it for a few days.

I smiled and nodded. He thanked me and left, pausing long enough at the gate to fold his hands together in one last namaste. I waved back. I closed the door and bolted it from the inside, thinking about the concluding lines of a verse that is written on the wall in Mother Teresa's room in Kolkata.

The good you do today, will often be forgotten. Do good anyway.

Give the best you have, and it will never be enough. Give your best anyway.

In the final analysis, it is between you and God. It was never between you and them anyway.

Books matter

*Books can be dangerous. The best ones should be labeled
"this can change your life." ~ Helen Exley*

As I was walking through the airport terminal, a bookstore display caught my eye. Piles of books with the title *Eat, Pray, Love: One Woman's Search for Everything Across Italy, India, and Indonesia* piqued my interest. I read the description on the back cover and wondered if there was anything in it for me. It seemed to be the story of a well-heeled woman from New York who had embarked on a year of self-discovery across continents.

To be honest, the prospect of going away to a new place for a fresh beginning was extremely tempting, although highly impractical. Unlike the author Elizabeth Gilbert, a divorced woman without children who could conceivably reboot her life as she wished, I was a woman with a child who was my first priority.

My goal was to find my bearings without uprooting her life, or at least try to keep the changes to a minimum. I turned over the book and looked around the busy bookstore, reluctant to part with it.

Books have always been my best companions. They have not only provided entertainment but also served as wise, nonjudgmental mentors whenever I needed advice. The problem with my situation was that I had not come across a single book to guide me or at least accompany me as I laid out the roadmap for the rest of my life. In fact, I had no idea how I had arrived at this unfamiliar crossroad. I certainly did not deserve to be in this predicament.

I read the back cover and blurbs once again, searching for a message, but there was nothing. There was too much going on in my life and I did not have the energy to step into someone else's drama. As I set the paperback down, I wished there was a book that could help me.

Sometimes, wishes come true in strange ways.

Two years earlier when we had returned to Hyderabad, one of the hardest things we had to do was to ask Uncle J, the elderly gentleman who was renting the upstairs portion of our house, to move out. My in-laws lived downstairs, and our plan was to renovate the upstairs unit and move in. This way we would have privacy while allowing Shreya access to her grandparents.

Uncle J and I only met briefly but had an instant connection when we first met. Although he was older than my father, as a fellow scientist, I had great respect for him and felt honored when he sought out my company. We talked about science, society, family, and faith. Uncle's humble demeanor and broad outlook in life drew me to him. There was much to learn from him.

A few days before he moved out, Uncle J invited me to visit the factory he had set up with his son. We made a day trip to the site, which was located on the outskirts of the city.

Uncle showed me around with great pride and explained the workings of various machines and their plans for expansion. His devotion to work, his depth of knowledge, and, most importantly, his ability to continuously learn inspired me. How lucky I was to have a friend who could bring out my higher qualities and aspirations!

When news of the rift in our family reached Uncle, he sent word through Raju, who had been hired on Uncle's recommendation, asking me to meet him. I accepted and Raju drove me to Uncle J's new house.

"How are you, Ma?" Uncle asked softly. His gentle words brought tears to my eyes. I didn't want to let him see it, but his kind eyes took in everything: the slump of my shoulders, the darkness in my eyes, the doubt in my demeanor.

Unlike others, Uncle was not curious about the details of our split. His concern was for me and completely genuine. He could sense my resolve but also my confusion. Like me, he wondered about the impact of my decision on Shreya. But he knew better than to suggest a reconciliation without addressing the cause. He knew I needed help, something intuitive but nonobvious.

"Why don't you meet my daughter-in-law, Susheela? She runs an organization that helps women. I am not sure what exactly she does, but a lot of young women seem to find it helpful."

Was she a therapist? A psychologist of some sort?

Counseling and therapy were not things that Indian families talked about or had faith in. Families were supposed to take care of themselves. Most conflicts were brushed under the rug or handled discreetly by elders or other well-wishers to avoid airing dirty linen in public.

Uncle gave me Susheela's phone number. I agreed to call, not sure I had the time or bandwidth to forge a new connection and spill my sad story to a stranger. Yet, I called—not with the hope that she would have answers but because I trusted Uncle and his genuine regard for my happiness.

When I called, I was not sure what Susheela would make of my reference. She invited me to come over to her office for a chat.

"I have to go to work from Monday to Friday," I said.

"We're open on Saturdays. Come in anytime," she replied.

The following weekend after dropping Shreya at her father's place, I stopped by Susheela's office. The place buzzed with happy anticipation. Women moved around with smiles, stopping to greet each other. Everyone seemed to know everyone else. A group was coming together in one of the rooms for some kind of a session.

Susheela welcomed me with a smile and closed her office door.

"I don't know why Uncle asked me to meet you," I started off, uncomfortably.

She wasn't fazed by my nervousness. Through a few strategic questions, she gauged my predicament. She handed me a book titled *You Can Heal Your Life* by Louise Hay.

"Why don't you read this book?"

I glanced at the slim paperback with a rainbow-colored heart on its cover.

"We have a two-day workshop at the end of the month that is based on this book. You can join it. It will help you," she said confidently.

I was not sure about a group activity.

What if it was a sharing session?

What if everyone else was happily married but had other issues they wanted to talk about? I was not ready to divulge details of my ambiguous marital status to a bunch of strangers, and I certainly had my hands full with my issues and therefore had no interest in other people's problems.

Susheela sensed my reluctance.

"Just try reading the book. You can call and confirm your appointment when you feel ready."

Relieved to be off the hook for now, I asked if I could pay for the book. It was clear that her organization was a business.

"Not necessary. Read it first."

I clutched the book to my chest as I descended the stairs, not knowing that I was holding a lifeboat that would help me navigate the choppy waters that swirled around me. My airport wish had been granted.

Signs, they say, are everywhere if you care enough to look for them. Yet sometimes you need a person to point them out to you. Thank you, Uncle J.

Don't judge

Don't compare your despair ~ Robin Roberts

A new kind of sameness seeped into our days.
Wake up. Send Shreya to school. Go to work. Return. Repeat.
Work kept me busy, but the charade of pretending that nothing was amiss weighed on my shoulders like a heavy coat.
During my first winter in Washington DC, I had to learn the life skill of staying warm, which involved wearing layers of clothing—gloves, socks, and a thick coat that made my shoulders droop and my neck hurt with its unpleasant weight. I hated having to wear it every time I stepped out, but I could not stay indoors forever either. To survive the chill of the unfamiliar freezing weather, I had to wear it whether I liked it or not.
In a roundabout way, I was doing the same now. In order to hold up a facade of functionality despite the inner chaos, I had to learn to protect myself. Leaving home required me to don the cloak of normalcy as a shield against intrusive questions.

It was uncomfortable, but I had to do it. If I shrugged off this pretense, I would risk exposing myself to curious onlookers and unnecessary gossip. If I continued with it, I had to accept the discomfort to protect myself from the unfavorable outer circumstances.

I knew it was not a permanent solution.

Nothing was permanent, even discontentment.

I had moved to Hyderabad hoping to save and strengthen my marriage with family support. What I had found was the opposite. Our frayed marital relationship had not been able to withstand even the tug of a faint breeze.

Everywhere I turned, it seemed that people were competently handling their life with ease, except me. They seemed to be members of a society who possessed a secret code that I lacked.

Hoping to wind down from another forgettable day, I picked up Louise Hay's *You Can Heal Your Life*. As I turned the pages, a small point of light began illuminating my consciousness. Soon, a bright flashlight turned on in a dark corner of my mind.

Much of what Hay said seemed to come straight out of my life: Bad things happened only to me. I was never appreciated. Everyone seemed to have a better life, or better luck, than me. How had she known?

I called and signed up for the two-day workshop that Susheela had mentioned. It wasn't cheap, but it was the best investment I could have made. The examples and exercises sowed seeds of understanding, introduced me to the power of my mind, and gave me something to do as I waited for my new life to take shape. At the workshop, I took a first stab at breaking the barriers of negative self-belief. It was a complete game changer that revolutionized the way I thought about myself and my life.

Instead of assembling the shattered pieces of my outer existence and inner reality into an incomprehensible structure, I learned to consciously create a new life.

What did I want?

To be self-sufficient.

To provide a stable home environment for my child.

To be peaceful.

What was stopping me?

My limiting beliefs.

My guilt and blame for all that had transpired.

My anger.

It did not matter if I was not "Mrs. so and so." It did not matter whose fault had brought me to this place.

The most important question was "What next?"

I had been given another chance to fashion a life of my choosing.

Being intentional about who I chose to hang out with would be the first step in the right direction.

At the workshop, I met Shobha who was assisting with the sessions. Later, she invited me to join a weekly discussion group at her home. A small group got together in her cozy living room to dig deeper into the lessons and deploy the tools toward our goals.

Even dark nights offer a sliver of light. One of the surprising benefits of separation was the oasis of time that I discovered on weekends when Shreya visited her father. Suddenly I was free, at least for the weekend, to do exactly as I wished. I put this gift of time, which had never been mine to claim, toward rebuilding my life.

For the first time in a long time, I realized how the stress of constantly being in firefighting mode had affected my life.

It wasn't just the two years since our return to India that had been demanding, it had been the same as far as I could remember, even before Shreya's birth.

Every single person deals with their own special trauma—there is no hierarchy of pain that makes one's suffering superior to that of others. We work from our own baselines, moving up in our understanding of how it all fits together.

In her memoir *Everybody's Got Something*, Robin Roberts says, "Don't compare your life to others. You have no idea what their journey is all about. That's why I always give people the benefit of the doubt; it's one of my rules to live by."

I finally gave myself the benefit of doubt. I put myself first.

In Shobha's study group, we were collectively dealing with wide-ranging issues—financial insecurity, health scares, worries about children, relationship breakdowns of various kinds. We were all hurting. We were all working to find the meaning in our misery.

I may have been the only one coming to terms with divorce, but I was not alone in having reached an impasse in my life that needed reengineering of a kind that required group support. We were united in our common wish to find a way of carrying our burdens by shifting the blame away from others and finding coherence within ourselves.

Adjacent to the room where we sat sipping cups of hot tea, I noticed a small open courtyard with a high ceiling, illuminated by a skylight. I could see rays of sunlight streaming in, lighting up everything in its path. I could not yet feel it's warmth from where I sat. But I knew it was there, within touching distance. The light at the end of this seemingly never-ending dark tunnel that

I had entered, was on the other side of understanding. The clarity I was seeking was within my reach.

I felt a sense of homecoming. I had found my tribe. A group of people committed to making sense of their lives but also intentionally moving in their chosen direction.

Without embarrassment, over the following months, I learned to share my slow, painful progress toward coming to a decision about divorce. It may not have been of direct interest to the group but perhaps they needed to hear it too, just as I needed to hear about the happily married couple who were dealing with financial woes, and about the chronic health issues that plagued someone who came from a wealthy family.

What I needed in terms of emotional support I took from the group. I gave them my story. They gave me encouragement. When someone spoke, we all listened—without interruption, without judgement. Occasionally, someone would ask a question. Or simply vent.

The lessons were embedded in the sharing, in the sitting in a safe circle that facilitated communication. Sometimes the group had an answer to a question, or a recommendation, or a simple solution to what had seemed to be an intractable problem.

We spent time reading chapters from another book, *Radical Forgiveness,* by Colin Tipping, a book that offered me an alternative explanation to why my life had turned out the way it had. Surprisingly, each member of our group was able to understand the reason for their own situations as well.

We tackled the exercises in the book, either alone or in pairs. We played a board game called Satori that playfully introduced the concept of radical forgiveness, a term that I learned to embrace despite my logical nature that sought explanations rooted in the world I knew and understood through my five senses.

Over time, I came to realize that I may never truly understand the sequence of events or confluence of factors that had brought me to this place. I had to accept that. I had to forgive myself and I had to keep moving.

Instead of reacting, I had to take a measured response in the direction I wanted to take. I could reassemble my life by picking up only those pieces that I wanted. There were no guarantees, but there was peace in knowing that I would be able to face the next detour when it arrived.

Walking therapy

A path is a prior interpretation of the best way to traverse a landscape ~ Rebecca Solnit

The large L-shaped terrace of my new home overlooked a frangipani tree in the front yard. The house was too big for just the two of us, but it had its benefits as well. The private gate that enclosed the yard provided a degree of separation from strangers, and the private terrace allowed me a safe, quiet space to mull things over at night after Shreya went to bed.

The full moon hung low on some nights, yellow and heavy with a promise of better days. On dark nights, the moonless sky reflected my somber mood. I often walked in silence, allowing thoughts to pass through me like ripples passing through still water.

Walking counted as exercise; I knew that. As a nonathletic, studious person, walking had always enjoyed the status of "most favored sport" in my life for reasons other than mere exercise.

Growing up back in Mumbai, my best friend Tejal and I had often walked hand in hand, two cool and carefree teenagers wearing similar clothes, stepping forward with a spring in our step that made our braids swing around our shoulders like pendulums. Some evenings we walked to the temple, on others we did errands or stopped for spicy street food when we had the craving and money to indulge.

Traffic fumes engulfed us as we navigated streets crowded with vendors pushing cartloads of bananas, people queuing up at bus stops, and beggars lining the pavement. We talked as we walked, trying to make sense of growing up and understand the world of adults while we contemplated our futures.

We didn't know then that she would get married young but remain childless, a regret that still stings. Neither could we have predicted my marital troubles.

As a young working woman in California, I walked during my lunch hour as often as I could. Stuck in a laboratory all day, mothering a baby in the evenings, and catching up on housework on weekends left few options for exercise. I strolled around the one-mile periphery of the triangular campus. Gentle breezes often blew around my face as I walked in my comfy Easy Spirit pumps, taking in the pleasant greenery of the beautiful site.

Walking helped my body lose some of my pregnancy weight and, along with yoga, enabled me to make peace with my decision to be a working mother without letting debilitating mommy guilt weigh me down.

The term "walking" denotes so much more than putting one foot in front of the other.

I hate being walked over. I detested walking on eggshells. I had walked out of my marriage.

And now I was walking into unfamiliar territory, walking toward new experiences. I was clearly not walking on air, at least not yet.

Even though I was not the first woman in the world to have left an untenable situation and an unhappy marriage, the path was not clear. As Rebecca Solnit would posit, no one had presented a "prior interpretation" for me in this situation. No one could. I had to find it for myself, a prospect that both excited and terrified me.

I walked along the edges of the terrace in slow measured steps, seeking answers.

Walking, as they say, is a way of being outside without having to talk to anyone. Sometimes silence, more than words, can provide solutions. It was a catalyst for creativity—not for creating a work of art but for creating my life.

Walking was not a passive act; walking was my moving meditation.

With each step I repeated affirmations:

The past has no power over me.
I am divinely guided and protected.
I am in the rhythm and flow of ever-changing life.
Life is simple and easy.

I expressed silent questions and stayed receptive for an answer, not sure what form it would take.

How could I keep my full-time job while ensuring Shreya was safe when she returned from school? I worried about her safety, but I also worried about my job. I was responsible for rent and all the other expenses for the two of us, now and for the long term.

My parents, although supportive, were living off of my father's modest pension. My brothers had their own families. My top priority was to maintain my financial independence.

Shreya's well-being and our financial security seemed to be mutually exclusive. Every time I rode this train of thought, I stepped out on the terrace.

Walking didn't solve the problem, but it gave me a way to keep moving. Walking didn't bring me to a destination, yet it gave me a way to negotiate the unknown. By holding space for my doubts, walking rescued me.

It gave me a respite from life and also a reason to continue with it.

Through walking, I learned to zoom in on the things closest to me, the ones with the most significance. Although the days seemed interminable, I became comfortable inhabiting an in-between space that was full of possibilities.

Later in my journey, walking would be instrumental as I pieced together clues and resources to reconfigure my career, which was very different from the one I had planned. But at this juncture, I took solace in this mindful pause that helped me collect myself emotionally so that I could present a cohesive facade to the world.

Eating well

*I love the process of learning a thing.
It's doing a thing I find so boring ~ Laurie Colwin*

On a sunny New Year's Day in New York city almost a decade ago, I had impulsively bought three beautiful hardcover books: a collection of short stories by Maeve Binchy, an author who wrote of life in Ireland; *Ordinary Miracles,* a novel by Linda Crew about infertility; and a cookbook, *Dakshin, Vegetarian Cooking From South India* by Chandra Padmanabhan.

After my PhD defense, I finally had time on my hands, which I decided to devote to reading (willingly) and to improving my culinary abilities (unwillingly).

In the first few weeks of 1995, I laid in bed, reading or staring at the ceiling, weighed down by a deep sadness. Crew's novel spoke directly to me. I pictured myself as Betsy Bonden, the protagonist who suffers a series of setbacks while trying to get pregnant, but in the end, has a happy ending.

Where was mine? Did I not deserve to have a baby? Two years after a miscarriage, doctors continued to insist that, physically, everything was fine.

"Ease up," they said, in their breezy, cocky manner.

How could I? After submitting my final PhD thesis before Christmas, I applied for jobs but had not found any. Getting pregnant was the only goal that I considered worth pursuing. I was listless and lost.

"Take care of yourself, " they said. "Eat healthy and make sure you get enough exercise."

The prescriptions sounded excessive and exhausting.

No one spoke of "getting exercise" in Mumbai. In the course of a day, I would climb up and down hundreds of steps at train stations and often run to catch a bus. The heat and humidity, my own high metabolism, and a body type that tended to lose weight faster than it gained, had allowed me to stay sedentary. Exercise was not a part of my vocabulary. Plus, I would always choose a library over a gym any day.

Healthy eating seemed like a sensible goal. Although simple homemade food was my first preference, I had acquired a taste for pizza and tacos, foods reserved for the occasions when we ate out while in the United States. My cooking skills were limited to what I had learned by watching Amma cook back home in Mumbai.

The gorgeous glossy photographs of familiar traditional foods in Chandra Padmanabhan's cookbook made my mouth water.

Fluffy *idlis* and fiery *sambar,* rice dishes and desserts, laid out in shining brass and steel vessels, and arranged for maximum effect on luxurious place settings. Given my lethargy, there was no way I could rouse myself to concoct these recipes. I shut the book and turned on the TV.

I scanned the channels until I came to the Food Network. Show after show featured delicious meals that were said to be simple to prepare—broccoli and cheese quesadillas, spinach and mushroom crepes, colorful pasta, and more. I was fascinated by the practiced movements of chefs who expertly sliced and julienned vegetables and assembled impossibly beautiful desserts.

I liked Lydia's Italian cooking, Yan Can Cook, and looked up Julia Child after hearing her name mentioned on many shows. What I didn't do, however, was try to make any of these dishes at home.

Binge-watching food shows helped me get through the day, but they didn't help me get out of bed and jump into the kitchen. Eating and cooking were two separate tasks. Cooking preceded eating, and it required motivation. My lack of appetite, both for food and for life, made it impossible for me to get excited about the recipes in the book or on TV.

Unlike that dark period of my life when I was obviously depressed, now I was just being lazy. Although I didn't admit it to anyone, separation had led to two pleasant side effects: in addition to the weekend break that allowed me to claim "me time" when Shreya went to her father's place, I was relieved from the burden of cooking for my family.

Of course, I had to cook for Shreya and myself, but it was not the same kind of pressure. As long as I made simple, kid-friendly meals, we managed just fine. Shreya was a slow eater but since moving to India, she'd widened her palate to include local favorites like curry puff and *pani puris*. Some days, we stopped by the local *chaat* place for *aloo tikkis* and called it a night.

The problem was on weekends when I was alone. Cooking for one didn't hold much appeal, eating alone at a restaurant felt too morbid, and I didn't like ordering in either.

I occasionally accepted invitations to friends' homes but didn't want to foist myself on them, knowing that their weekends were reserved for family time, errands, or socializing.

I turned to Chandra Padmanabhan's book and looked at the hopeful inscription that I had written on the inside cover page.

"Towards new beginnings!"

Had I really hoped to turn into a gourmet chef by buying a cookbook? I had often skimmed its glossy pages, admiring the small portions of food arranged in attractive bowls, surrounded by elegant accessories, and captured in the best light. Why didn't my cooking look this good?

The answer was simple. I had approached cooking as I approached most tasks: something to tackle, master, and check off from my list. Cooking was a skill I wanted to acquire, even though it was not an innate strength.

Plus, I had done it because of an ulterior motive.

The way to a man's heart is through his stomach—I had heard that maxim hundreds of times. It had even been offered as advice to bolster my faltering marriage.

If only I could cook better, I had thought naively, *I could save my marriage.*

After a long day spent in the laboratory setting up complex experiments, I would rush home to concoct a meal from scratch, assuming the traditional responsibility of a wife. I cooked one multicourse meal a day, usually in the evening. Focusing on efficiency over taste, I learned to assemble a simple meal of one vegetable, one dal, and rice, a meal that was tasty, if not fancy, within an hour.

Food was necessary for survival. I enjoyed eating small, perfectly flavored portions of freshly cooked food, but it was not the highlight of my day. Given everything on my plate (pun intended), I could not justify devoting more time to a memorable meal. Who remembers every meal that they ate anyway?

Certainly not me.

Despite the optimistic declaration in the cookbook hinting at new beginnings, my good intentions ran aground fairly quickly. A goal, no matter how trivial or lofty, needs the momentum provided by the conviction that it is being pursued for the right reasons.

The issue of my cooking ability (or lack thereof) blew up into a big problem, and although I could not figure it out then, I see it clearly now:

I did not lack ability. I lacked interest.

Although I didn't mind admitting that I wasn't the greatest cook or hostess, I hated being evaluated on that front alone. We met other couples wherein the wife was a reluctant (or terrible) cook. The husband often helped in the kitchen, and sometimes took over the complete responsibility for cooking. Their marriage seemed to be doing fine.

My logical brain was confused. If a woman's cooking ability was not a factor for marital harmony, why was I putting so much effort into a task that wasn't of much interest to me?

With this basic conflict lodged firmly in mind, every attempt I made to improve myself in the kitchen backfired, despite my best intentions to the contrary.

As a child, I was a fussy eater. I ate sparingly, but I liked to eat, as long as the food was perfect—in flavor (not too spicy), texture (not too pasty), color (not too pale), and various other parameters on which I judged every meal.

Like many of my generation, during my childhood I had little or no access to factory-produced processed food. We always ate freshly cooked meals at home. Amma was a great cook but also a practical homemaker. Everyone had to eat the meal cooked for the day.

Since she cooked a variety of dishes, each one's favorite food would appear in a system of random rotation. While I didn't care for eggplant or fried snacks. I enjoyed desserts. Regardless of preference, I ate small portions of everything.

Watching Amma in the kitchen, I concluded that cooking was an inescapable part of a woman's life. Amma, however, had let me off the hook during my teens.

"You learn everything quickly. You'll learn to cook quickly as well," she assured me. Instead of excelling at the basics of the routine rice and vegetables that formed the staples of wholesome, homemade meals, I attempted the more challenging tasks—rolling out circular discs of dough that fluffed up into airy *phulkas* and ladling out batter on a hot griddle to make crisp, golden round *dosas*. These small wins gave me a sense of accomplishment, but I soon got bored once I mastered the task.

Was it my ambivalence to cooking in my early years that made me resent having to take on the responsibility for the kitchen in my married life? Or was it because I had many other things to do outside the home that made me come alive, pushing cooking down the list? Or was it the lack of support and encouraging feedback?

Why not test the hypothesis now as a separated woman alone for the weekend? If I cooked what I loved to eat, without piling any expectations on it, would my concoctions taste better?

I began with one-pot meals—*khichdi, pulao,* lemon rice. Then I added *aloo paratha, masala dosa,* and grilled vegetable sandwiches to my repertoire. On weekdays when time was scarce, Shreya and I enjoyed spaghetti with tomato sauce that we poured out of a jar, or we assembled pizza on a pan using a store-bought pizza base. Our meals were simple but fun and yummy.

It wasn't that difficult to cook. Or to eat well. The key was to do it with love, for myself and for my family.

Returning to Yoga

Practice what you know, and it will help to make clear what now you do not know ~ Rembrandt

On the day I left my husband's home, I did exactly what I did every single morning. I laid out my yoga mat and went through the sequence that I had fine-tuned over two years.

In California, I attended classes at my workplace or at a yoga studio, which was a short drive away. In India, there was no class within walking distance or at a time that matched my work schedule.

Although I preferred a live class with an experienced instructor, I had no choice but to put together a series of asanas that infused me with energy. It was a premium I paid each morning for good health. Who knew that the steadfastness of my practice would also strengthen my mind?

My introduction to yoga began a few months after Shreya's birth—first as a coping mechanism but later it evolved into a fitness strategy. Returning to the laboratory eight weeks after delivering a baby had not been easy.

My body felt like a shapeless, semi-deflated balloon. I dragged myself to work each day with sleep-deprived eyes that seemed permanently encrusted with sand and took naps at my desk when I thought no one was looking.

"It's always easy to spot the new moms," my colleague said with a wink and a smile one morning, pointing to the tell-tale drool marks on my left shoulder.

My supportive boss, who pretended to look the other way when I was slumped in my chair, showed me a poster announcing a trial yoga class. At the office gym, I was the only Indian woman (other than the instructor) in a class of about twenty, predominantly female, employees.

"You had to come to America to learn yoga?" smirked the woman on my right.

"I had to be stressed enough to need it to come here," I replied haughtily.

My initiation into the ancient practice of yoga began on that tart note. Despite the initial difficulties of performing even the simplest of moves, I would get a happy buzz after each yoga class. The hour-long session soon made me feel like a floating helium balloon. I slept better, lost weight, regained my stamina, and somehow felt happier about life in general.

Over the years, I attended various types of yoga classes at private studios and gyms, learning minute posture adjustments and nuances that made a difference. Each instructor's teaching style influenced my practice.

While I still preferred a group session, I began to enjoy my morning hour of solitary practice in Hyderabad as well. My daily yoga practice had made me stoic and sensible, allowing me to plan my exit with a clear mind instead of running out in anguish from my husband's home.

Weeks after moving into the new house, I woke up one morning with a clear command ringing in my mind: get back to yoga.

My life was radically different since I first ventured into yoga practice, yet deep in my cells I understood that the only way I could manage the unsettling present was to hold on to those aspects of my former life that had held me steady in the past. As a new mother, yoga had come to my rescue. And now, as a single parent, yoga was exactly what I needed.

The two upstairs bedrooms had no furniture. Not even curtains. Sunlight streamed in from the east-facing windows each morning, flooding the rooms with fresh possibility.

One Saturday morning, I carried my well-worn yoga mat up the stairs to the smaller bedroom and laid it out strategically by the window. Through a flimsy curtain of green foliage outside, I could look into the neighbor's house across the narrow street. I had gathered that a couple with two young daughters lived there.

I heard a car door slam moments before I saw the lady of the house returning home from her night shift at a call center.

I began with sun salutations. My body was stiff. Even the basic forward fold felt foreign. Yet I knew that muscle memory would kick in if only I could stick with it long enough.

I followed the familiar sequence gingerly, not wanting to stretch beyond what my tightly curled body was capable of on that sunny morning. I needed to move, but I also needed time—time to find my new rhythm in this place and in this phase of life.

It felt good to move in a familiar way given the newness of everything else.

"When I'm practicing on my own, how do I know if I'm doing it right?" I had asked my first yoga teacher.

"It is very simple. Check how you feel. If you feel better—lighter, more comfortable, more peaceful—that means you are doing it right."

If I used the same yardstick to judge how I felt about my life in general, I knew I had done the right thing. The asana practice confirmed what I already knew. Despite the challenges that lay ahead, there seemed to be a lightness of spirit that suffused even the more complex aspects of my life as a single parent, something ineffable that I could sense but not grasp.

What was it? This fleeting fragrance of a feeling that I could at once recognize but not capture? I wished I could hold on to it for longer instead of having mere glimpses of it.

Life is movement. Life is action. As a child, I was known as the girl who was easily bored. I was always found doing something, even if it appeared to be a superficially passive activity such as reading. When my mind was engaged, my body was also alert.

As an adult, I found ways of keeping busy. My brand of spirituality involved action. As a firm believer of "karma yoga," otherwise known as yoga of action, the dynamic nature of the asanas resonated with my basic nature. I had integrated yoga smoothly into my life.

But now I needed something else.

"How about meditation?" A friend suggested.

To me, sitting still meant dullness, lethargy, and monotony. And life, ever so obligingly, had thrown me enough action and drama to keep me busy. Every moment spent "doing" meant less time for silence or for self and less opportunity for introspection.

But my life was not the same now. Neither was I.

On days when I was at a loose end, tension curled around my neck and temples like the tentacles of an octopus that had made a permanent home around my shoulders. If I sat quietly, worries about the future took center stage, and if I turned away, the past roared with a litany of all the things that I had messed up. How could I sit still and stay sane?

Silence scared me. Loneliness too. My childhood in a small apartment in a big noisy city had set the precedent and the preference for chaotic cacophony in the safety and anonymity of urban life. Going inward was as frightening as being lost in the woods. I was afraid that dark thoughts—guilt, blame, self-pity—would emerge from the shadows of the recesses of my mind where I had pushed them.

Meditation was supposed to be a way of sitting with your thoughts. I was not ready.

"No, thanks. I don't think I can sit still for long," I replied to the well-meaning friend, who, wisely, did not push it.

Carrying on

Change is one thing. Acceptance is another ~ Arundhati Roy

The worst thing about your life falling apart is that the world takes no notice.

On some days, I felt as if the rubble of my life covered me in an ever-increasing pile. Yet the sun rose every day, bringing with it non-negotiable deadlines at work and a list of activities at Shreya's school that I could barely keep track of. Shreya was an organized and cooperative child, bookish and shy.

"I have to wear a saree, tie my hair up in a bun, and go to school on Friday," she announced one morning. Although a bit surprised that Shreya had volunteered for a dance performance, I was pleased that she was trying new things at school, despite all the upheaval on the home front. It had been a good decision to minimize her stress by letting her stay in the same school.

I often wore sarees to work and had a decent collection. But I wasn't sure how to dress an eight-year-old child with six yards of fabric.

The material had to be light enough for her slender frame, plus it needed to be tied snugly to prevent unraveling during the dance. While I struggled with the mechanics of the costume, Shreya had other worries on the morning of the show.

"I don't feel good," she wailed.

She dawdled over her milk. Her face looked sicker with every sip.

"Why?" I asked.

On school days, Shreya usually woke up eager to go to school. Every night, she organized her backpack, made sure her uniform was ironed, and laid her shoes out by the door. Last night she had packed her uniform into her bag knowing that she would need to change out of her costume after the dance.

She had become used to the new school routine from our new house and had made friends with kids on the school bus.

Her face was scrunched with worry. Had something happened at school? Had her father said something over the weekend? In a few short weeks, Shreya had learned to compartmentalize her split life between her homes. She seldom spoke of what she did there, unless it was to narrate some incident with the puppy or a friend who lived down the street.

"I don't want to dance today," she said.

We had thirty minutes to get her into the saree, comb her hair, and walk to the bus stop. It was too late to back out now.

"I thought you wanted to participate. Everyone in the group needs to do their part, right? And you know all the steps," I said.

She nodded, unconvinced, and got up.

"Drink your milk," I reminded her. She didn't like milk, but we had agreed that she would drink it in the mornings. Given her general mood, I knew she would not eat any breakfast.

"I don't want to drink," she replied. I gave her a warning look and pointed at the clock.

She gulped the rest of the milk in a hurry and reluctantly went to her room where we had kept the saree and accessories ready.

She looked pretty with the flower-patterned saree that I had folded up and tucked high and tight at her waist so that she wouldn't trip on it. Her soft, silky hair took a little bit of effort to curb into a bun. But I looked fondly at her as I walked her to the bus stop.

"I don't want to dance," she repeated again, tears poised at the tip of her long eyelashes.

I squeezed her hand, confident that she would be fine once she saw her classmates. The excitement of the event would overcome any fears.

The bus was late that morning. As the minutes ticked by, Shreya's face got darker with worry.

"I don't feel good," she said again, before suddenly throwing up.

The milk that she had swallowed earlier came out in one long spout. I stared in disbelief.

I had underestimated the extent of her discomfort, having focused solely on getting through the morning and then through the day that awaited me at work. I was not prepared for this detour. I couldn't scold her; I could only blame myself for being oblivious to my child's misery.

Shreya was crying but calmed down soon after she emptied her stomach. I pulled out the bottle of water from her backpack. Remarkably, her saree was unsoiled. She rinsed her mouth and took a few sips of water. Her face relaxed.

"Do you want to go to school or stay home?" I asked, even though I knew it would be difficult for me to reschedule my day at work on such short notice.

"I want to go," she replied, much to my surprise.

"If you go, you will have to dance," I reminded her.

She nodded. I sighed, relieved, but proud that she was willing to carry on. I waved her off that morning knowing she would be okay.

I walked back home and threw myself on the bed, hot tears pouring from my eyes. Why did it have to be this way? I had no buffer. Everything was sliced so thin: my time, my patience, my sanity. Even a minor change of schedule could upturn my well-planned day in a moment. It wasn't fair. Anger and self-pity poured out with my tears.

I looked at the clock and wiped away my tears. I had thirty minutes to get ready for work. I had to learn how to be stoic like Shreya.

How had this little child already learned that life must go on despite minor inconveniences and major setbacks? That what she does every day counts? That when she ventures out of her comfort zone she must embrace the excitement even if it is tinged with fear?

All through that day, I kept going back to our shared morning moments. Shreya had mirrored my feelings about my life. I had walked out of a dysfunctional home, not knowing what was involved in setting up a functional one.

Some days, everything seemed to be under control, but on others, I felt nauseated. And every so often, I just wanted to throw up my hands in surrender, give up, and crawl into bed. But that was not an option.

On some level, Shreya understood that her friends were counting on her for the success of the group dance, which meant she had to show up at school despite her discomfort. I was doing that on a daily basis—for Shreya, my colleagues at work, and for myself.

No one cared that my little world had come crashing down. I could cry if I wanted to, but I still needed to hold up the small piece of it that depended on me.

Prioritizing self-care

Beauty is not caused. It is ~ Emily Dickinson

A simple but powerful exercise in *You Can Heal Your Life* involves gazing at yourself in the mirror and looking deeply into your own eyes. When I first attempted this exercise, I found it unsettling if not downright unpleasant. The task was easy: just look into your eyes, with love and compassion, as you would look at someone else who needed it. The challenge was in holding your gaze for the longest possible time without turning away.

I tried to trick myself by doing it while brushing my teeth. My eyes looked puffy on most days. My hair was a mess. There were dark circles under my eyes, and my eyebrows were like little overgrown bushes.

Every few seconds, I had to bring my attention back to my eyes. I studied their brown-black irises looking back at me, wondering what (or who) lay behind the veil of my eyelids.

Was I in the mirror or was I looking at the reflection in it? Who was that tired person with a busy day ahead?

She seemed exhausted, overwhelmed, and in need of care. I felt sorry for her. My heart was heavy with compassion. She needed support, a kind word, a loving touch, and a break, but all I could do was send her good wishes and heartfelt sympathy.

I could not guarantee her a happy future, but I could ease her load by meeting her gaze and wordlessly transmitting positive vibes.

I love you. I support you. I am always there for you.

Some mornings I cried. On others, I smiled—at my foolishness and my optimism. Yet, on most days, I felt stronger at the end of the exercise.

A strange thing happened after a few weeks. My eyes seemed brighter, my face fresher. A subtle shift had occurred at the subconscious level and floated to the surface. I felt, dare I say it, good?

"Come with me. I am getting my eyebrows done. Let me introduce you to Seema," Kumari said one Saturday afternoon.

I tagged along with Kumari, not sure if I was in the mood for a visit to a beauty parlor. The whole setup of such salons intimidated me. The supercilious women with their immaculate hair and nails, the attendants in uniform who milled about as if in possession of secret knowledge, and the huge bill at the end of each session made me uncomfortable.

However, during my mirror exercises, I couldn't help but notice the state of my eyebrows. They certainly could use some attention, so this was as good an opportunity as ever.

I met Seema, a homemaker with an entrepreneurial spirit who had started a home business. She had converted one room of her home, tucked away in a corner of a row of houses, into a professional-looking beauty parlor. The room was small but well-equipped. A well-lit rectangular mirror on the wall and two reclining chairs occupied most of the space. Seema had a pleasant face and received us with a welcoming smile. She chatted amicably with Kumari as she attended to us with minimal fuss, no upselling, and no false promises. I liked her brisk manner and professional attitude.

"Come anytime, but please call first," she said, as we paid her. I took her number, just to be polite.

The next day, the neat soft arcs of my eyebrows stared back at me in the mirror, a reminder of the few minutes I had devoted to my physical appearance. I had been conscious of my health and supported it by eating well and continuing with my yoga practice and regular walks despite the upheavals.

I had also kept up with my work. But, somehow, I had deprioritized self-care activities that focused on my body alone. I firmly believed the cliche that beauty was skin deep, and I certainly didn't consider myself superficial.

Why then did I feel better today with the small adjustment to my face? Was it because I looked better? Perhaps. But I felt better too. It wasn't the act itself but the fact that I had taken the trouble to put myself first. The eyebrows had taken only a few minutes to reshape, but those were minutes that I had set aside for myself.

Maybe it was time to give my body a break too and give it some kind attention—a pedicure would surely feel good, as would a nice scalp massage to revive my limp hair. How about a facial? There was no end to the things people did to look better, and I would never be the type of person to sign up for all of it, but I could at least make a beginning.

I called Seema and made an appointment.

Prevailing, again

The most difficult thing is the decision to act, the rest is merely tenacity ~ Amelia Earhart

Like many Indian families, my family sometimes turned to astrology for guidance during times of unexpected difficulties. Although I did not care much for idle predictions, there were days when I wondered if my choice to move ahead in life as a single parent would succeed.

I felt I was doing the right thing, but I had nothing to anchor the feeling to. I had no idea about the future. All I had was the knowledge that I had faced difficult situations in the past, situations that had demanded flexibility and a leap of faith, and I had triumphed.

I recalled one of the biggest challenges I had faced during my PhD days.

Midway through my doctoral program, my academic advisor announced that he would be leaving the university. It wasn't unusual for untenured assistant professors to quit. Whether they moved to other universities or switched to corporate life, it was always bad news for the students.

Research work involved grants that were specific to the principal investigator (aka professor), which meant the funding source for your own efforts would go away along with the guidance and mentorship you expected. For those professors who left academia altogether, as mine was planning to do, I would have to downsize my dreams and stop at a master's degree.

I felt cheated. It had taken a great deal of mental adjustment to chase a PhD in the first place. I had begun my graduate student life in the United States with small steps. Initially, I had enrolled in a master's program as had been agreed at the time of my wedding, and I had been unsure of my ability to pursue a doctorate. In my extended family, except for a great uncle who had left India and pursued a PhD in London, no man or woman had shown interest in such a pursuit.

A year into the program, two professors sat me down and invited me to switch over to the PhD program, based on my academic performance.

I accepted their offer but not without seeking advice from other married Indian women like me who had chosen the same path, postponing plans of motherhood and making other adjustments and sacrifices to invest in their own education. I did the same. And was thrilled with my decision.

I loved my lab. I enjoyed my work. I saw value in what I was doing for its own sake, notwithstanding the benefits that might accrue in the future. Plus, I felt fully alive in a place of learning, surrounded by a diverse student body and renowned professors who embodied humility and wisdom, an inspiring and irresistible combination.

"You can choose to continue here if you like."

My advisor broke the news of his departure over a casual lunch in the medical school cafeteria located across the street. He noticed my uncharacteristic silence as I took in the impact of his words.

"How?" I asked.

"There is money in the grant. It should be enough to support you for a couple of years. I can advise your research remotely, but you would have to pick a professor in the department to formally be your guide," he said.

I was intrigued by this offer. Financial and practical aspects aside, could I do it? Research, write, and complete my dissertation with minimal supervision? My face must have reflected my self-doubt.

"I have already discussed this with Dr. A, the head of the department. He is confident that you can do it," he said.

I was surprised. I had kept a low profile during the two years I had been in the department. Unlike other students, I showed up for classes, worked in the lab from 9 a.m. to 5.30 p.m., and left with the administrative staff at the end of the workday.

I was an outlier in my peer group, most of whom showed up late, kept erratic hours, and hung out in the labs even on weekends. How had Dr. A concluded that I had what it took to complete my thesis with remote mentorship?

The first time I had entered the department, I met Dr. A, a tall gentleman with piercing blue eyes. He sat in a corner office wearing a white lab coat and holding a sheaf of papers in his hand. He didn't seem ruffled by the sight of an Indian girl with a long braid wearing a green salwar kameez, red bindi, and Nike sneakers at his door.

When he unfurled his legs and stood up to ask me in, I couldn't help but notice how tall he was. He explained the process of admission into the graduate program and excused himself to bring me a brochure. I looked at his messy desk and bookshelf lined with leather-bound books. I noticed a few copies with his name along the year of my birth on the spine. He had graduated with a PhD from this university the year I was born!

I remained in awe of him ever since that first meeting. His soft voice, gentle demeanor, and the quirky way he positioned himself next to the blackboard to write with his left hand had only increased my respect for him.

I felt relieved at the thought of Dr. A as my guide. I could proceed with my plan, having the financial support for my research and guidance from my advisors as needed. It wasn't ideal, but it certainly was doable. If Dr. A felt I could do it, I felt confident that I could do it. I clutched at that straw and ploughed ahead.

Less than three years after that conversation, I completed my dissertation. A combination of money running out, space constraints as a new professor arrived to replace the one who left, and my own issues with infertility conspired to speed up my graduation. The going had been tough but I had prevailed.

Those troubled years had been a time of growth, just as my current life seemed to be. I was at a fork in the road of my life where it was clear that certain plans were not going to materialize the way I had hoped. Yet within the whirlpool of the issue lay the kernel of the solution.

I could not turn to Dr. A for support or a vote of confidence now, but I did have proof that I would be able to survive this detour.

Back then I had always thought that it was the focus on the goal of a PhD that had helped me prevail, but now I could see that it was my willingness to learn, evolve, and tackle the challenges that had come after the decision to continue in my graduate program despite the unconventional terms.

No one is ever guaranteed a smooth life, so to expect

as much is foolish. To be daunted by the challenges thrown at me was natural, but I knew what lay ahead was not insurmountable.

I felt confident that I could figure out my life as a single parent. I did not have a crystal ball to predict my future success, but I had proof from my past efforts. For now, that was enough.

Attitude of gratitude

*What good would it do to allow annoyance
to interfere with gratitude ~ Katrina Kenison*

I had a pretty hardbound notebook with a pale green cover and a square cutout showcasing a yellow sunflower that always made me smile.

Where and when had I bought it? Probably on a whim at some unnamed mall in the United States.

Had I planned to write things of importance on its thick, smooth paper on the day I picked it up? I couldn't remember.

One night after Shreya went to bed, I idly turned the pages and found that I had made some entries. A few paragraphs at the back and many pages at the front of the book.

The first entry was dated January 30, 2001:

"I guess the last (almost) day of the first month of a new year in the new millennium is as good a day to start this journal as the first of any year."

I wrote about a conversation I had heard on *Fresh Air with Teri Gross*, one of my favorite shows on the National Public Radio.

I loved listening to NPR as I drove to or from work or while doing errands. On that day, the host had interviewed a neurologist who had recently written a new book about the brain and its relation to our sense of self—our identity and its precise location in the brain.

Why did I write about this?

Was it a watered-down version of an ambitious new year's resolution to journal or to capture things I had heard or read in the course of an ordinary day?

The next entry was on Valentine's Day, entailing a cynic's rant on the commercial aspect of romantic love, on the meaningless annual rituals that cover up thoughtless behavior for the rest of the year—an honest peek into my feelings on the topic.

The two entries pretty much summed up the state of my mind and my marriage.

To save myself from excessive negativity, I frequently sought out opportunities to elevate myself mentally. Through books and activities that helped me soar over the disappointments of my home life, I escaped the dark depth of my loveless marriage that could have otherwise sucked me into depression.

Reading always calmed me down, but I had not considered writing as therapy.

Other than the mandatory essays written in school, my science education had not demanded any writing beyond scientific publications during my PhD days.

My first foray into writing for myself had been a side effect of my pregnancy. It had been an almost miraculous journey to get to the second trimester. I began typing into a Word document on the home computer at night.

Soon the impulse to write gathered momentum and I continued to write for the first two years of Shreya's life.

What had begun as an intimate exercise in documenting her babyhood had expanded into an exploration of my own feelings.

After her second birthday, I began writing essays on topics that were foremost on my mind—topics that resonated with me as a woman, a mother, an employee—yet I avoided writing about my role as a wife.

The first essay that I felt confident enough to share was titled *"Contractions and Contradictions,"* a piece about motherhood and the conflicting feelings it brought up. I sent it to the *San Jose Mercury News,* not expecting a response. After all, I was not a trained journalist or writer.

When I received an email informing me of their acceptance along with a request for a photograph of Shreya and me, I was both incredulous and scared—yet happy at the prospect of sharing my story with strangers who read the newspaper.

That first success led to other small wins. *India Currents,* the Indian American magazine in the Bay Area, ran a few of my essays and short stories the following year, and one short story won an award.

When we decided to move back to India, I pitched the idea of a monthly column about our experiences as nonresident Indians returning home to the India of a new millennium. When the editor accepted my pitch, I was thrilled to continue the association despite the distance.

Writing, however, turned into an additional cause of friction in my already-fraught marriage—or at least the publication part of writing did.

When a friend from California visited Hyderabad and invited us to a lavish celebration of the birth of his twins, we met his parents, who had spent a few months in the Bay area helping to care for the newborns.

"Ranjani is the writer whose articles you read in *India Currents*," my friend introduced me to his father as I folded my hands in a respectful namaste.

"So, you are the scientist-writer who describes the experience of returning to India so beautifully," he began. "I used to wait each month for *India Currents* to arrive so that I could read your article."

I blushed, taken aback by this unexpected praise but pleased to meet at least one reader who liked what I wrote. I looked at my husband to share the moment, but his mouth was set in a hard line. He turned the conversation to something else, and in his careless dismissal my pleasure evaporated and left behind a lingering, bitter residue of resentment.

When my first piece appeared in the paper in 2002, it occupied almost half the page and included a large photo of me holding four-year-old Shreya in my arms, which was taken on our trip to Maui.

We were both smiling, Shreya displaying her crooked teeth with lips painted a characteristic bright pink from the lipstick samples I'd accumulated with my moisturizer purchases. Even the people who hadn't read the article had seen the picture. I received several phone calls and voicemails from friends and colleagues who had found it cute. But Shreya's father said nothing.

I briefly considered using a pen name to maintain anonymity, but the thought of hiding behind a pseudonym didn't appeal to me. I continued to submit other general interest articles, which would often be read by people in our social circle.

Each time, some version of the reaction to the first newspaper article would occur. When extended family or friends appreciated my writing, it resulted in unpleasant conversations or, worse, complete silence from my husband, who offered no support whatsoever.

One of my articles about elections in India appeared on a California news page and was later quoted in the *Times of India*. When a colleague brought this to my attention, I was thrilled. After all, I was no journalist, so to be quoted in a national newspaper was no small feat. Yet, the only reaction at home was displeasure, and to make matters worse, my in-laws shared their son's antipathy toward my creative efforts, especially when my work brought me visibility in the public realm.

To minimize disagreements, I stopped sending out my writing and refused offers to contribute to magazines and newspapers. Among the many small injuries that slowly crushed my spirit each day, hurtful comments about my writing shut down the small window of creative exploration that had sustained me.

Like any plant that suffers without life-affirming nourishment, my writing withered and died.

The rediscovery of my green book with its hopeful sunflower was a reminder of the old me who had tried to save herself by writing. Here was a typical entry.

> 15 Feb 2001
> 1. Sunny skies
> 2. Swing in the park
> 3. Making up silly words with Shreya
> 4. Attending evening class at the U. of Santa Cruz
> 5. Reading Simple Abundance

I had picked up the book *Simple Abundance: 365 Days to a Balanced and Joyful Life* by Sarah Ban Breathnach a few months ago. I loved the book's simple format of short chapters, one for each day of the year. Flipping through the pages served as a daily reminder and a lesson in the ways in which I could foster habits and practices that could lead to a richer life.

Was my green notebook purchased in response to the gentle encouraging words from *Simple Abundance?*

Books had always come into my life when I needed them. And this one had made enough of an impression to make me take action. Instead of focusing on what I did not have, I decided to do what I could. The easiest thing was to write down what I was grateful for every day.

My days were monotonous, boring, tiring. Were there at least five things to be thankful for? I decided to find out by writing.

21 March 2001
1. My clean and clutter-free apartment - thank you Lupe, for coming over every Wednesday afternoon to clean and transform my home
2. A bouquet of daffodils from the farmer's market
3. Silently chanting shlokas while driving
4. The sweet smell of Shreya's freshly shampooed hair
5. Lunchtime walk with a friend

I didn't write every day, but I read through several similar entries. By writing what I was grateful for, I learned to look for things that made me smile. I retrospect, I could see that there had been much to be grateful for, even on days when Shreya was more dependent on me, when I spent long tiring hours in the laboratory at work, and when home was a battlefield.

My current life was far from perfect. Clearly, my pretty gratitude journal and its entries had not prevented the catastrophic failure of my marriage. But the habit of focusing on the good had helped me get through the days once. Could it work again?

I needed to find out if I still had a motherlode of gratitude buried somewhere in my psyche. I would have to first clear the debris of disenchantment, clear the path and allow that small trickle to come through.

At a macro level, I knew that although I was separated, I was now free of the daily drama that had once sucked the life out of me. The need to constantly watch for his moods. The intense desire to please. The stress of not knowing what the day would hold, what trigger might lead to an argument or a standoff. The absence of volatility itself was a great blessing.

I no longer had the notional partnership of a spouse but I was also free of the expectations that went along with having one. I did not hope or pray for support. I did it all, as I always had.

For now, I was alone at the forefront of a new phase of my life. My parents were a phone call away. Soon they would arrive to help me physically and emotionally until I got my feet firmly planted.

Until then, I would resume the practice of counting my blessings:
1. *Shreya's presence makes me strong.*
2. *My house is safe and comfortable.*
3. *I have a job that pays me a good salary.*
4. *My friends are always willing to help me.*
5. *I am healthy.*

Helping others

~~

You drown not by falling into a river, but by staying submerged in it ~ Paulo Coelho

Despite the difficulties, my new home seemed suffused with a lightness that was hard to describe. Was it the novelty of a space that I had not lived in before? Or was it because the air was cleaner, unsullied by past disagreements and disappointments?

A place can be a living, breathing thing. It can shimmer with joy or with maleficence. I couldn't really call it joy, but certainly a loosening of sorts—of clenched teeth and rigid expressions, of a tight knot at the center of my being that kept me in a constant state of readiness for fight or flight—had certainly occurred.

But there was a lopsided balance to this new ease as well. I had been fortunate to have a considerate boss who was not nosy and easygoing neighbors who had provided contacts and references to help me settle in. I went to work, Shreya went to school, and all was well. Mostly.

At work, I maintained a facade of being supremely capable and self-sufficient, although I knew in my heart the hollowness of such a shield. I was in my late thirties and this was the first time in my life that I had truly left the presumed security of my father's/husband's home and created a life without the kind of background support that I had always counted on.

In my office I came across many women in their early to mid-twenties who had chosen to take up a job in Hyderabad, a city where they did not know anyone. Some had come to the city as students and stayed on, whereas others had been recruited at college campuses and chose to begin their careers here. I was in awe of these clear-headed strong women.

On one Friday evening, I stayed in the office later than usual, knowing that Shreya had been picked up from school by her father. As I walked out, I noticed a colleague still at her desk. I knew the office bus had left almost an hour ago. Transport options from our workplace, which was located on the outskirts to residential neighborhoods in the city, were few and unreliable. What was she still doing here?

Samantha was bent over her desk, her hands covering her head.

"Hello, Samantha? Are you OK?" I asked.

She raised her head slowly. Her eyes were glazed with pain. The left side of her face appeared swollen. Her forehead was hot.

"You are burning up. What happened?"

"I had a wisdom tooth extracted two days ago. It's hurting a lot. I have had a fever all day," she replied.

I knew Samantha had moved to Hyderabad for this job and lived with a roommate.

"You probably have an infection. Where's your dentist?" I asked.

"Near my home," she replied.

"Let's go then," I said, helping her gather her things. I asked Raju to bring the car to the front of the building. Despite her pain, Samantha managed to give directions to the dentist's office.

Within a few minutes, the dentist diagnosed the source of the infection, cleaned up the area, and prescribed an antibiotic.

"Are you Samantha's sister?" The dentist asked, curious to see me, an older woman in a saree, hovering over Samantha.

"She is my boss," Samantha replied, her words slurred by the ball of cotton in her mouth. The dentist looked surprised but didn't say anything.

We stopped at a pharmacy on the way to Samantha's home where I bought her the recommended medicines. She looked much better than she had all day and refused help when I offered to walk her upstairs to her apartment.

I returned home that night feeling as if the scales had been turned in some way, even if it was just by a tiny measure. In a small way I had been able to repay the many kindnesses I had received in the past few months, and by doing so, had completed the circle of giving and receiving that makes up our lives.

Our role in the grand scheme of things is very small and may seem inconsequential, but there are times when the full import of what we do is revealed to us, often at the most unexpected times. I would have been alone in my spacious home on any other Friday evening, heavy with feelings of abandonment and sorrow.

Yet now I was entering it with a feeling of unbearable lightness.

I had put aside my burden, at least for a moment. I had seen another's pain. And that had made all the difference.

Avoiding negativity

If you don't like something, change it. If you can't change it, change your attitude ~ Maya Angelou

Denial can be quite powerful.

Shreya came home in tears one day.

"This boy in my class, he called me stupid," she sobbed.

When she calmed down, she told me how the self-proclaimed leader of a group project bullied everyone on the team. Shreya was not comfortable with confrontation and as a rule she preferred to wait and watch.

"Do you think you are stupid?" I asked. Shreya shook her head.

"Just because he said it, does it make it true?" I asked.

"No," she replied and looked at me, understanding dawning across her face.

Words have power. When we internalize things that people say about us, those words often become our beliefs.

For her sake, as much as mine, I wanted her to believe what I had just said. Just because someone said something (negative or hurtful), I didn't have to make it my personal truth.

When did I make this my mantra? Was it as a little girl, trying to match my physical might against my brothers who had teased me about being weak because I was a girl?

Or was it when my suggestions were not taken seriously at work because I was a woman?

Or when an unkind relative made a remark about my childlessness in the years I suffered from infertility?

I couldn't remember the exact turning point. A succession of events and experiences had made me find my survival mantra long before I became the woman who had walked out of her marriage.

At a subconscious level, I had decided to refuse to accept the words of others as the absolute truth. What I had chosen instead was to stay away from negativity and pessimism. Yes, life was hard. Yes, the world was not fair. Yet there were people who valued me and supporters who enabled me. In their eyes, I could see the reflection of my authentic self:

The professor who was convinced that I could complete my PhD thesis with minimal supervision.

The boss who offered me flexibility, knowing that it would make me a committed employee.

The neighbor who helped me settle in my new house without prying into the reasons why I was renting a big house with only a small child and no husband.

Unknowingly, I had built a tribe of believers, a community of supporters, by moving away from those who sucked away my life energy and left me depleted and defeated. Instead, I was moving toward those who had my back and supported me. And I, in turn, reflected their generosity out and toward those I could help and encourage.

There's always a choice and that choice begins with words—the stories people tell you and the stories you tell yourself. How you choose to build the foundation of your life will determine how well it stands up against the naysayers who try to trip you up.

Like Shreya, I too had come across doubters and so-called well-wishers who were most interested in digging up dirt and gossip, insinuating lies, and spreading falsehoods. My initial irritation and anger had finally boiled over into exasperation. I could not change them, but I could avoid them.

And so, I followed the exact advice I gave Shreya.

"You know you are not stupid. His words don't matter. Don't be afraid to do your part. You will only be proud of the things you do, not the things you were afraid to do because of what someone said."

Accepting invitations

Solitude is fine but you need someone to tell that solitude is fine
~ Honoré de Balzac

On most days I felt like a porcupine and on others more like a bear.

In response to perceived threats, porcupines raise their quills, whereas bears prefer to hibernate as per the season. As a woman living alone with her child, I felt protective toward our vulnerable situation.

Every person who stepped into our home, whether it was the guy who came to install the telephone, or the plumber who fixed a leak, would innocently ask, "Where is sir?"

It wasn't their fault; a standard nuclear family was supposed to have, at a minimum, a man, a woman, and a child. Mine did not. Suspicious of their motives, I would respond with a casual "Why?"

Did he think a woman could not understand the basics of operating a home appliance? Was he simply curious? Or did he have an ulterior motive?

My mind worked in overdrive, assessing perceived and real threats and trying to figure out a way to keep us safe from known and unknown terrors.

At a team-building seminar at work, the human resources head ran an ice breaker exercise, which he claimed would bring teams closer.

"Get to know your team members by asking questions about their family," he stated with conviction.

"People feel seen when you inquire about their life outside work. Begin with basic questions like "Are you married?" or "How many children do you have?"

I was aghast. Not just at the question but my response to it.

Before my separation, I didn't mind such questions since my life had largely been lived on the beaten path—one husband, one child. Although I missed the American way of life that prized privacy, I knew that in India people tended to ask probing questions even in casual encounters. It was more a cultural reflex than unnatural curiosity.

Yet now, even the most fleeting interactions were fraught with reminders that my life was different. I had lost the anonymity that came from conformity.

To answer such questions from strangers I had two options: tell the truth and open myself to further questions or give an ambiguous answer that fudged reality.

Over time, I fine-tuned my algorithm. For people I didn't expect to meet again, I would say "married, one child." It was the truth. In life, I was separated, yet legally I was still married.

For others who may have a means of verifying my response, I would mention that I had one child, allowing them to conclude that there must be a husband. Most times, people seemed satisfied.

On the rare occasions when chatty handymen showed up, I stayed mum, letting them figure out the answers themselves.

"Sir is posted outside Hyderabad."

"Sir works abroad."

"Sir is traveling."

They filled in the silence with plausible guesses.

I did not correct them, although I did wonder how Sherlock Plumber concocted these options. It didn't take long to figure out the reason. As it turned out, I was not the only one in the neighborhood with an unusual home situation.

A gynecologist lived at the end of our cul-de-sac with her two children because her husband had a government job that involved frequent transfers to rural outposts. Kiran, who lived next door, had a husband who traveled frequently for work and was hardly around.

The most outgoing pair of kids in our street were not siblings but cousins whose parents lived in a small town in Uttar Pradesh, but the children lived with their grandparents in Hyderabad.

The fact was that families came in all shapes and sizes. It was humbling to realize that I was being myopic and as judgmental as everyone I liked to accuse. It was me who had labeled my situation as being nonconforming and therefore an object of curiosity.

At work, most colleagues didn't question my status, assuming that my family situation was the same as the time I had joined two years ago. While I had opaquely informed my boss that "I would need some flexibility to handle a personal situation," I had not provided details.

But it was different on the home front. In response to every provocation, I would get my quills up, jump into flight or fight mode, prepared to defend myself and my child. I was exhausted by constantly being on high alert. The only option was to withdraw from social interactions as much as possible.

When Shreya went to her father's place on weekends, I remained at home, closed from any unwanted encounters. I was reluctant to meet new people at that point in my life. Every friendly hello would be followed by questions that made it difficult for me to provide a truthful answer. What use were such shallow interactions or friendships forged on half-truths or complete omission of major facts about my personal life?

A decade ago, I had been in a similar situation during my season of infertility.

The natural progression of marriage was parenthood. After the first miscarriage, the doctor informed me gently that early trimester miscarriages like the one I had experienced were common—almost fifteen percent of pregnancies end like this.

My logical mind absorbed the fact, yet my heart didn't accept it as something that could happen to me. How could a physiological event be explained purely in terms of science and statistics? There was an emotional consequence to my loss.

"Relax," they said. "You will get pregnant again."

Months passed with no difference in my situation. My anxiety rose. I detested meeting people who would innocently ask us when we were planning to have a baby, implying that we were the ones obstructing the process.

For five years I used the excuse of completing my PhD as a cover-up. Most people presumed that I would have a baby once I graduated.

But two years after the fact, I was still childless.

Friends and relatives persisted with their kind inquiries. Is there a problem? Did you get your horoscope checked? Meet this specialist. Consult this astrologer. Perform this *pooja*. They couldn't have known about my deep desire for motherhood, a yearning that overshadowed any accomplishment I could claim as mine. If it was up to me alone, I would have had a baby by now, maybe two. But I was being thwarted by an unkind universe.

I could not rile against the inquisitive well-wishers. I could only avoid them. So, I did.

The path of least resistance led to hibernation. I refused to attend parties or gatherings of any kind, particularly baby showers or birthdays of our friends' children. The simplest way to save myself was to decline every invitation. I made excuses about being busy with work or travel.

In retrospect, I could see that hiding had not helped. All I had succeeded in doing was alienating myself from well-meaning friends, including the one who would finally share her infertility story, give me the phone number of her reproductive endocrinologist, and insist that I meet her. Her kindness and generosity in sharing her story would lead me to the person who would later help bring Shreya, the light of my life, into the world.

Hiding was probably not the best thing to do now either, but the impulse to protect myself from unwanted questions was strong. How could I ignore it?

Radha was the one constant support in those early weeks even after I moved out of her home. We met at work almost every day where she checked on my well-being.

"Why don't you and Shreya come over this weekend?" Radha asked. She was having a birthday party for her younger child. I could not refuse.

Shreya was delighted to attend a party with balloons, bubbles, and a bouncy castle. I made small talk with the other moms, most of whom seemed engrossed in the proceedings or busy chasing after their little ones.

Other than general inquiries about which school the children attended, there wasn't any prying. I relaxed and bit into a slice of the delicious cake that Radha had baked. The kids squealed with delight, their little party hats bouncing on their heads as they ran around.

For a moment, the dark cloud that followed me dissipated. The laughter of children fully immersed in the pleasure of the moment pierced through and dispelled the bubble of depressing thoughts.

I remembered my paternal grandmother, the one who had borne ten children and many hardships in her life, who, despite her lack of familiarity with English, would occasionally say, "this too shall pass." If she could endure the tribulations of her hard life, I could survive this phase of mine.

Finding beauty

Give the present the gift of your full attention
~ Maggie Smith

There was something unusual about the location of our new home. Although I was still intimidated by its size, usually on the weekends when I was its sole occupant, I had begun to notice the unnatural stillness of the quiet lanes, late at night and in the early mornings. My narrow cul-de-sac was an oasis of silence.

Every house was identical to the other, strictly following building codes within the property. Many of the neighbors owned their homes and tended to their tiny gardens with great care. Large trees planted many years ago had matured and now generously provided shade and fruits.

The Mumbai highway lay a few hundred meters away. At dawn, trucks rumbled along honking, their jarring sing-song tones serving as wake-up calls to even the most stubborn sleepers. Dogs barked in response and chased cars or other invisible targets. Yet, when I walked on my terrace at night, I could not detect any signs of city life.

There were no tall buildings as far as my eye could see, even though Hyderabad was booming, sprawling outward and skyward, its once-laidback facade morphing into a metro like any other.

Would this be my forever home? It felt so temporary. I was paying rent to live in a house that felt large and alien. Like an intermission during a long movie, I was waiting for my "real" life to resume. I had never penciled in such a detour in any list I had made for my life.

Like me, Shreya loved to make lists. A year ago, when my brother's family had visited from Kolkata, she had compiled a list of places she planned to visit with her cousins: the zoo, IMAX theatre, Charminar, Golconda Fort. After each outing, she would check off the item and happily anticipate the next one.

"She has taken after you, making lists," my brother observed wryly.

It was true. Perhaps my super-focused approach to life—the desire to maximize the moment, to mine each opportunity, to make the most of every single day—had rubbed off on her. There was merit in being organized. Making a list ensures you'll get more done, generally speaking—I'm sure there are studies to support my hypothesis.

The downside of such a habit is that it requires you to focus so sharply that you only see the items on your list and you forget to take in the big picture. As you check off the tangible items, you miss the tiny details that make life beautiful. Everything you do does not need to have a practical use; it's important to make space for beauty. This was a lesson I had not learned yet.

Like all children, Shreya lived in the moment regardless of the circumstances of her life. The highlight of her eight-year-old life was Sparky, her pet dachshund.

She reveled in his company and loved him unconditionally. She had a way of focusing on what was good in her life.

Once, while listening to her excited description of Sparky's antics after returning home from her father's place, I recalled a conversation I had with her almost five years before.

We were on our way home from a swimming lesson in Santa Clara, and Shreya was uncharacteristically quiet. From her car seat, she seemed to be looking out pensively. Perhaps she was tired, I thought. It had been raining all afternoon and finally the sun was peeking through the clouds.

"Look! There's a rainbow," she shouted suddenly, straining against the seat belt as she turned toward it. I looked through the windshield but could not see it.

"Where?" I asked, not taking my eyes off the road.

"Here," she insisted.

Through the rearview mirror, I could see her pointing out the window.

"I can't see it," I said, sad to have missed it.

"You have to look with my eyes if you want to see it, Amma," she said, settling back into her seat.

After a long day at preschool followed by a fun but tiring swimming lesson, she had stayed open to receiving the unexpected beauty of a rainbow that had shown up in her window.

Back then I had always been caught up in my busy life, weighed down by the burden of monotony and unfinished tasks. Upset by the unfairness of it all,

I had closed myself to the beauty of daily life. Yet there was much to appreciate if only I opened my eyes. Her words were a wake-up call for me then—and maybe I needed to look through her eyes yet again.

Through a strange set of circumstances, I had stumbled upon an oasis of silence in a bustling city. Even as people went about their daily lives, bargaining with the vegetable vendor, preparing their meals, getting their children ready for school, I was surrounded by pockets of beauty.

In *Keep Moving*, poet Maggie Smith uses the term "beauty emergency" to describe moments when you have to stop everything and look. She was right.

There was rain, but there were rainbows too. The parrots that perched on the tree outside my gate rose up and flew off in brilliant patterns each day, even if I chose to gaze at my feet. What would I gain from wantonly ignoring the beauty in my life?

I took a moment to inhale the strangely intoxicating fragrance of the jasmine that I could not see but only experience. What else was I missing at this moment?

As Shreya had said all those years ago, I had to look through her eyes to find the beauty in my life. It would take effort, but it could be done.

Chasing motherhood

There are places in the heart you don't even know exist until you love a child ~ Anne Lamott

Dressed in a dark blue Charter Club suit and a white shirt, I stood in a conference room with a smooth oval mahogany table. It was a cold, rainy day three weeks after my twenty-seventh birthday. I looked around at the members of my thesis committee—all men, mostly Caucasian—and had the realization that I had come a long way, literally and figuratively, to be in this room, where moments earlier I had successfully defended my PhD dissertation.

"Congratulations, Doctor!"

Every student and staff who entered the room shook my hand. A chilled bottle of champagne was opened, and the golden liquid poured into small plastic cups. A layer of bubbles, like tiny transparent pearls, clung to the sides of my cup as I inhaled the mildly fermented odor and politely smiled.

Through the double-pane glass windows that lined two sides of the rectangular room, I could see the barren trees, stripped of their autumn finery by the seasonal rain.

The evening rush hour progressed as cars accumulated on Martin Luther King Jr. Boulevard, which separated the University of Maryland, Baltimore campus, with its prestigious graduate schools, from the red-bricked housing projects. I raised my cup following the cue of Dr. A, my academic advisor, and took a reluctant sip.

Since my arrival in the United States, I had spent almost five years in this highly respected school in downtown Baltimore pursuing a doctorate in a scientific field. Members of my thesis committee signed the page that marked more than just an end to my field of study.

To my family, it signified me as the only woman in the family to have persevered this far. To me, it indicated the completion of a journey that was signaled by an incident that occurred when I was four years old.

My first teacher, "Padma teacher" as she was known to parents and children alike, was a plump woman who wore colorful sarees and a large red *bindi* in the middle of her forehead. Her preschool, located across the street from our apartment building, was actually a multi-purpose room, square and spacious, with a smooth wooden floor that made hollow creaking sounds in response to the stomping feet of boisterous students.

In preparation for kindergarten, all kids were expected to learn to read and write the letters of the English alphabet. The ability to write cursive letters was used as a test to rank students before handing out the annual report cards. Parents were expected to help their children practice their writing in notebooks lined with red and blue at home, paying special attention to the complicated curls of the upper and lower cases of the letters J and Y.

I struggled to demonstrate this skill during the test and therefore missed the first rank. On the way back, I wailed as my mother tightly held my hand to cross the busy street navigating around stray dogs and speeding black and yellow taxicabs.

"Why are you crying? You know all your letters, we can practice writing during summer holidays," she spoke in her most patient voice.

"I want to be first," I shouted back, upset that she did not understand this simple fact. It did not matter whose fault it was. The result was what counted. I was second and that was simply not acceptable. I wanted to be first!

As I grew from an overachieving preschooler to a motivated college student, one character trait that remained constant was my unchanging drive to be first, to learn more and faster than my classmates.

My presence in the rectangular conference room with its plush carpet and oak bookcases was the consequence of a love of reading and academics, my fiercely competitive spirit, and the ambition to set standards for myself that were higher than those set by others. It was a seminal moment: one of victory and of glory. But as I stepped out of the school on that cold winter night, all I could think about was what I really wanted but didn't have: a child of my own.

The image of woman as mother is universal, not specific to any culture. But in India, that image is elevated to iconic status by a society that puts marriage and motherhood at the core of a woman's existence. As a young girl, I may have doubted my ability to live and work abroad, but I had never doubted my ability to bear children, a belief that was reinforced by the fact that I had never met an Indian woman who was childless by choice.

To me, children and marriage were synonymous. And here I was, a young married woman who had not produced a child six years after marriage. Although society had not yet pointed fingers at my barren state, I had fallen short in my vision for myself as a mother.

I had always set and achieved high personal standards for my academic life, yet in the childbearing arena, I failed to accomplish what others were able to do without much effort or assistance. I saw my miscarriage not as a common medical event but as a tremendous personal failure.

Failure tests even the best partnerships, and our marriage was not immune. The cracks in our relationship showed up soon after the loss of the pregnancy. He didn't inquire about the reasons for my prolonged sadness or why I declined invitations. If I burst into tears for no apparent reason, he chose to avoid me altogether.

My inability to get pregnant meant that we would be childless, a setback if not loss for our marriage. I thought of it as our joint tragedy, yet it dawned on me that he interpreted it as my problem alone. I was confused by the discovery that we were not truly a team.

Three months after my PhD defense, hurt by his indifference and finding myself slipping down a road where nothing in life seemed to be of value, I decided to go home to Amma. Back in India, I felt safe and loved in my childhood home, though it was not easy to escape the well-meaning interference of family and friends.

So much of the "why" of life is a mystery. When logic fails, karma fills the gaps. Prayers and interventions in the form of religious *poojas* began.

In my struggle with infertility, a mountain of suggestions were flung my way: pray to Krishna for a lovable child like him. Chant this *shloka*. Visit that temple. Suspending logic, I prayed and chanted as instructed from the comfort of my mother's home, where she fed me my favorite foods and masked her shock at my emaciated state.

My in-laws consulted an astrologer who suggested *naga pratishtha*, a religious ritual to fix the flaw in our horoscopes. For maximum benefit, the ritual had to be performed at Rameshwaram, a sleepy town located at the southern tip of the Indian peninsula, to pacify the gods and reap the fruit of offspring.

The *pooja* was not a trivial undertaking. It was a two-day event that began with a dip in the Indian Ocean. I pulled the edge of the saree over my head as we walked barefoot to the beach in the sweltering heat. I stepped into the water beside my husband, acutely aware of the weight of my water-logged saree tugging at my hips.

I took a deep breath and dipped my head in the water. I made sure that I was completely immersed in the purifying water as I prepared for the intense rituals that followed. I obeyed all instructions sincerely, a single thought weighing heavy on my mind: there shouldn't be any lapse on my part, no lack in my devotion. I must have the blessings of the gods for a child of my own.

The previous evening at Chennai, on our way to Rameswaram, a well-meaning cousin had asked, "As an educated woman, why are you going ahead with this charade of the pooja?"

Her question was not unreasonable, yet I was still taken aback. Being scientifically trained had nothing to do with my decision to go ahead with the pooja just as my being educated had nothing to do with my being childless.

For the elders in the family, the pooja was a way to appease the gods and they wished me well. It is not doctors and deities that cure but faith. Riding on the blessings of my elders, I discarded the heaviness of my longing into the ocean, feeling a momentary lightness as faith carried my unspoken desire to the higher powers. But we were not done yet.

For a nominal fee, a young man, dressed in a white shirt and cotton lungi wrapped around his waist, pulled buckets of water from each of the twenty-two holy wells and emptied them on our heads. I cringed as the water hit me and evaporated with a sizzle. I wondered: am I washing away sins of the past in this cleansing ritual?

The next morning, without eating breakfast, we walked to the home of the priest who would perform the main pooja. A group of bare-chested priests sat around a wood fire in a dark room, chanting mantras.

As the hours progressed, the air filled with the smell of incense and dense smoke from the offerings poured into the sacred fire, mingling with the vibrations of the chants uttered in unison. I passively followed instructions until the point when all my thoughts and movements became concentrated into one solitary plea: *"Please God, let me be a mother."*

The world stopped. I ceased to exist as a woman with a prayer.

I became the prayer, the smoke, the fire, the air, the sound.

In that moment of surrender, I handed over my destiny to the unknown universal force that guides each of our destinies.

After the rituals in Rameshwaram, I lingered in Mumbai, reluctant to return to Maryland, even though spring had arrived and the cherry blossoms around the Jefferson Memorial were in full bloom.

Amma urged me to return, gently pointing out that I would need to be in the same place as my husband if I wanted to get pregnant. One rainy afternoon, I sat across from Amma, sharing a pot of tea.

"Are you ready to go back?" Amma asked.

"I think so," I said.

"Promise me you will take care of yourself. I don't want to ever see you as I did when you arrived here—all skin and bones. Instead of being happy for achieving your dream of a PhD, your eyes were dead."

"I promise. I won't ever go down that road of self-pity again. I know what I have and what I don't. I have to make my life work because I have so much. I am lucky. And grateful," I said.

Amma and I locked eyes. She could see that I was not mouthing empty words but uttering a prophecy or a prayer. In either case, I was making a promise, to her and to me, to hold my mental well-being above the vicissitudes of life.

Two years after that conversation, Shreya was born.

Her birth itself was proof that miracles happen. Holding her in my arms that first morning when she finally arrived, slick and bloody after a long labor, I felt the physical exhaustion slip away, followed by exhilaration and then a sobering moment of silence as I made a commitment to her to keep her well-being at the forefront of all my future decisions.

Dodging depression

Do not let what you cannot do interfere with what you can do
~ John Wooden

Ten years after my impassioned plea with the gods, which was ultimately granted, I learned that the universe has a wicked sense of humor.

The months before my parents' arrival in Hyderabad were not easy. Each day I worried about whether the maid would show up in time to pick up Shreya from the bus stop. Whenever possible, I declined late evening telecons, and I dreaded quarterly meetings and office events that included drinks and dinner at five-star hotels in the city—occasions that my colleagues looked forward to as perks of a corporate job.

I was barely holding together the threads of my life as a single parent during the week and any excursion from the planned routine threw me off.

One morning Shreya woke with a shriek.

"The mosquitoes are biting me," she cried.

While the pesky mosquitoes were a constant problem

all over the city, the green cover around our new home provided a thriving environment for vicious ones that seemed to take great pleasure in biting my child.

One look at the red rashes on her hands and back was enough to convince me that mosquitoes were not responsible for this, whatever "this" was. I had a sneaking suspicion that I didn't want to say aloud.

At the old house, I had taken Shreya to the doctor who lived down the street, a woman whose daughter was Shreya's friend. I had no idea about a doctor in this neighborhood.

A taxi pulled up outside our door to drop the neighbor from across the street who was returning from her night shift at the call center. Assuming she would know a local doctor, I rushed out to intercept her before she entered her home.

"Hello. Sorry to bother you, but can you please suggest a doctor or pediatrician nearby? My daughter is not feeling well."

She graciously provided me a phone number and gave me directions to the nearest clinic. It would open in two hours. There was nothing I could do but wait. I informed my boss that I would be late.

The pediatrician, a young man with a relaxed bedside manner, took one look and confirmed my doubts.

"Chicken pox. Common childhood disease," he declared. "Don't send her to school and use calamine lotion for the itching. Nothing to worry about."

His peppy take on the diagnosis did nothing to alleviate my worries. I wasn't worried about the disease so much as I was about its impact on my workweek. It would take Shreya at least a week, if not longer, to recover and be allowed to resume school. What could I do until then? I could not leave her alone at home. I had to stay home.

After suffering the tribulations of infertility, Shreya's conception and birth had both brightened and complicated my life. Amma had arrived to help me through the early months, but once she left, I had struggled with mommy guilt for leaving her with Catherine, the babysitter, while I went to work.

It seemed unfair that I could not have both a fulfilling work life and enjoyable motherhood without feeling selfish for wanting it all; I craved quality time with my baby. For some reason that I could not articulate, it had also seemed imperative for me to advance my career.

I could not have known then that those years of work experience would lead me to my current job, which in turn would provide sustenance for the two of us through this phase of life.

Shreya slept fitfully as I fretted. The week was full of important meetings and deliverables that required my presence. Working from home was an alien concept, and no technology would allow me to be present in two places simultaneously. I had no choice but to take time off from work.

I took deep breaths as I watched my child sleep. Soon I would instruct the maid to pluck a handful of neem leaves from a neighbor's yard. It was supposed to help with the itchiness that accompanies scab formation. Shreya had been immunized against the virus back in California, but it was not a guarantee of complete protection. I hoped she would exhibit mild symptoms but have robust lifelong immunity after this episode.

Still, I couldn't help but feel defeated.

After fourteen years of married life in the United States, I had moved into what I considered "our house" in Hyderabad, hauling with me all the physical and emotional baggage of the years we had spent together. And now, three months after moving out, I had no clarity about my future. Without the support of family, the lynchpin of arranged marriages, I had rented a house, managed to keep my job, keep Shreya in the same school, and somehow hold my life and sanity together.

But this last straw almost broke me. I didn't think I could hold it together any longer.

Catherine, a licensed home day care provider had been my savior, support, and inspiration during the first five years of Shreya's life. At the young age of sixty-five, Catherine cooked fresh meals for the children in her care, cleaned her lovely home in Los Altos, and swam thirty laps in the pool every evening.

"How do you find the energy to do all this?" I asked her.

"I grew up during the second world war in Scotland. When I moved to the United States, I had to figure things out on my own. It was not easy. I changed jobs and pursued several careers in my life. When I became a single parent, I knew that I had to use my skills and my smarts to keep us afloat. I did not have the luxury to be depressed."

Catherine was made of hardy stock; she had been a teacher, a secretary, and a real estate agent at different points in her life and was a practical, no-nonsense, efficient woman whose words were tinged with common sense and the wisdom of her lived experience.

I was grateful not just for the care and love that Catherine showered on Shreya as part of her job but also for the daily interactions with her where I learned small details of Catherine's life.

All the women of Catherine's age group that I had known in India until then were either grandmothers to be feared or, even worse, irrelevant old women to be ignored. While they had been through their share of struggles, most presented themselves either as victims of their circumstances or as gatekeepers of the lofty patriarchal standards they had internalized.

Catherine had seen the world and experienced hardship, but she had also figured out a way to survive, crafted a philosophy that worked for her, and practiced it on a daily basis. She was true to herself and unlike anyone else I had ever known.

I wept silent tears as I gently stroked Shreya's back, pausing to feel the gentle breaths course through her body. Her illness forced me to pause, and I could not ignore my disappointment about the way things had turned out. But I also knew I did not want to be defined or defeated by it. I had been handed a deck of cards, and I had to play the game with what I had. My biggest blessing was Shreya.

Early motherhood had been a rocky road, just as married life had been prior to Shreya's arrival. But Shreya had served as a beacon in my stormy life, always shining a light on what was important, engaging me with her needs and her antics, reminding me with her smiles and childish statements. Right now, she needed my care. Work could wait. I, too, needed support in the form of my own mother who would arrive soon. Until then, I would have to hold it together.

In the gentle rhythm of her rising and falling breaths, my tears eased up.

III

MAKING IT WORK

Excavating the real me

The privilege of a lifetime is to become who you truly are
~ C. G. Jung

Who am I?

In the months since leaving my husband's home and particularly in the days before my parents' arrival, I asked this question of myself almost every day.

So many of the labels that I had accepted over the years described relationships: daughter, sister, wife, daughter-in-law, mother.

In the in-between phase of separation, was I still a wife? Could I check the box for "married" even though I didn't (and did not want to) share a house with my estranged spouse?

If I stripped off the labels that did not fit, who or what would I be?

I was still a daughter, a sister, and a mother. Why then did I feel so bereft?

The rationale for getting married at a young age was based on the assumption that the couple would grow together and evolve as a single, unified unit. But wasn't this premise inherently flawed?

Basic gardening knowledge tells us that plants located adjacent to each other in the same soil, with similar exposure to sunlight and equal access to water and nourishment may grow at different rates and in different ways.

From my own experience, I knew that despite being raised in the same home by the same parents, my siblings and I were very different—in personality and temperament, in our views and opinions, and in our dreams and ambitions for the future.

How could I be expected to evolve at the same pace and in the same direction as a stranger with whom I had tried (and failed) to build a mutually enabling relationship?

Most of the couples I knew had come together through an arranged marriage. My marital experiment was expected to succeed simply because "everybody goes through this and makes it work." Yet no one bothered to mention that, in marriage, like in the stock market, the caveat "past performance is no guarantee for future returns" held true.

My paternal grandparents were married in their teens, sight unseen, as per the prevailing custom. To me, they appeared to be an inseparable pair. They were old, kind, and always pleased to see their large brood of children and grandchildren gather for festivals and family events.

"Don't you think Avva is taller than Baba?" I asked my mother after we returned from one such boisterous gathering, observing Avva, my grandmother, whose regal bearing and strong personality contrasted sharply with my grandfather's meek, hunched demeanor.

In general, a wife was shorter than her husband. This was true with my parents. My maternal grandmother was tiny, not quite five feet tall. I was sure that her husband, my late grandfather, had been taller than her.

Yet here was a couple—whose genetic stock I had inherited—who seemed to buck the trend.

"Avva was thirteen when she got married. She probably grew a few inches after the wedding," Amma replied.

My Avva, a stoic but smiling woman had given birth to nine children and brought them all up to adulthood alive and healthy at a time when infant mortality was the norm.

She had scrimped and saved and fought to educate seven daughters and see them settled into their own families. Like a towering banyan tree protecting her offshoots until they were mature enough to plant their own roots, Avva certainly had done much more than just grow a few inches after her wedding.

In my teens, I had noticed only the superficial differences between my always-on-edge Avva and my easygoing Baba, who relied on his competent wife to manage their household.

But now I had different questions.

Had Avva wanted anything different? Despite very limited formal schooling, she could read and speak multiple languages, cook, sing, and sew. But what about her ambitions that were not related to family responsibilities? Did anyone ask her? How had she maintained sufficient interest and overlap with the stranger she had married? Had they truly grown together?

Adversity can be a great unifier, a stimulus that helps people bind together with a secret glue. My grandparents certainly had faced many difficulties, including the loss of an adult child and chronic lack of money. They had cleaved together. But tough situations can also rip people apart.

In my marriage, we had faced many challenges—infertility, illness, job loss, two major moves to and from the United States. There were certainly enough opportunities to test even the most devoted couple. We had never been cohesive, not even in the early years when life had flowed more smoothly. Each subsequent struggle had further worn down our resolve to make it work. We may have succeeded as individuals, but we had failed as a couple.

Instead of coming together, we had drifted apart. We addressed discord through a combination of prolonged periods of silence punctuated by occasional angry words. Interactions, if any, were minimal, and focused only on our child.

Over the years, frustration and resentment had accumulated to a point of despair.

I could not take it anymore and yet I shed tears for the loss of a long relationship and for a distant future that may have included our daughter's graduation, and perhaps her wedding and grandkids.

I grieved for what was yet to come. But I grieved more for what I had lost: myself.

I may not have grown in inches as my grandmother had, but I had certainly allowed marriage to change me in fundamental ways.

Without much instruction, I had figured out how to thrive in each unfamiliar environment—first in the United States and then upon our return to India. Like a vine twisted around a pole, I had repeatedly contorted myself to fit into the label of good wife and daughter-in-law. All of this had come at great personal cost.

I rarely smiled. I never cracked a joke for fear of offending. I hesitated to make plans for movies or travel without permission. I seldom bought things for my home on a whim. From buying our next car (which I drove) to donating money to our local NPR radio station (which I loved), I deferred to a husband who didn't really care.

I had declined writing opportunities that had come my way because drawing attention to myself was frowned upon.

Who was I really?

A scientist. A writer. A mentor. A friend.

When I stripped off all the labels, I was a person who had the right to pursue a life of purpose that was in alignment with my core values.

Loss comes in many colors. By walking out of my marriage, I had forfeited the benefits of being a "Mrs." But what exactly were those benefits? A false sense of being included in a larger family unit even though the effort to actually fit in was excruciatingly painful?

I thought about the ancient Chinese practice of binding a girl's feet so that they remain tiny. My feet were free, but my spirit was not; it was caught and constrained and silenced.

My duty was to free myself from the limiting beliefs that I had soaked up from society. The subliminal messages had insidiously taken up residence within me to such a degree that I wasn't sure if they were my own thoughts or foreign concepts that I had internalized over the years. My clarity was corroded.

Yet the feeling of things not being right had persisted until I could no longer swallow it. Or even breathe.

By walking out, I had chosen life. That was always the right choice.

Who was I? I couldn't answer that question.

Who could I become? Anyone I chose to be.

I could take the next sixteen years to figure it out, if needed. Learning takes time. First, I had to unlearn. Next, I had to uncover the real me.

Going with the flow

Bloom where you are planted ~ Mary Engelbreit

The callousness of life infuriated me. How could the sun rise every day, pretending as if nothing was remiss?

The vegetable seller called out every morning, offering a selection of seasonal produce—carrots and radish, cauliflowers and beans. Cars honked. Stray dogs barked. A cousin got married. My niece was born in California.

Shreya's school progressed as it always had: Tuesday test, Friday assembly, parent-teacher meetings. My work moved ahead—timelines, deadlines, meetings.

I put on a good show. Not particularly prone to irrational bouts or weepiness, I powered through the days, not knowing when (or if) there would be an end to this in-between phase.

Only the frangipani tree in my yard seemed to share my sadness. It began to shed its flat, smooth-edged leaves, just a few a day at first. Then many more. Tall but not lush, the tree was the centerpiece of my front yard. I had appreciated the delicate fragrance of its pale yellow petals, which were soft and thick but bruised easily when handled, just like my fragile inner state.

The frangipani's almost barren branches alarmed me. Had I destroyed it? I didn't particularly have a green thumb, but I watered the few plants that I had acquired with the house. A mango tree in the back, a few flowering bushes at the side, and this majestic frangipani tree that towered above everything else.

Was my bad luck harming this mature tree that held the place of honor in the courtyard? What else could be the reason? I wasn't having much luck with the rest of my life anyway.

"Is my tree dying?" I asked Bahadur, the gardener cum handyman who responded to random requests.

"Madam, this happens every winter. Don't worry," he replied. "You wait, in a few months, the leaves will return and also the flowers," he replied in his usual confident manner.

As a bonafide city slicker with no prior gardening experience, I wasn't convinced. I turned to trustworthy Google.

I learned that frangipani is a deciduous tree with simple smooth-edged leaves on fleshy branches. They lose their leaves in the winter and stay dormant during the colder months. It doesn't need to be watered until it shows leaf growth in the spring.

Bahadur didn't know Google, but he knew the ways of the natural world. What fertilizer works best? How to mix an effective blend of natural growth promoters? What to weed out? What to leave alone?

"What should I do now?" I asked, eager to help things along in my own determined way. Surely there was something I could do to speed things up.

"Nothing, madam. Nature knows how to take care of things. You just wait and watch," he said, amused by my disappointment.

The days passed with an irritating sameness. Nothing really happened.

School. Work. Weekdays. Weekends. Morning. Night.

Sometimes, after dropping Shreya at her father's place, I would visit the temple and chant Vishnu Sahasranaman and return home with a sense of calm that carried me through the lonely weekend.

At other times when the large house felt empty, its loud silence resonating with my inner loneliness, I went over to my colleague Shailaja's place. There was always a bed in her spare bedroom and a smile on her face as she opened the door. Sometimes we ordered pizza and watched TV or cooked a simple meal and stayed up late talking.

Like King Canute, who commanded the waves in the sea to stop, despite my best intentions, the world marched to its own rhythm, unaware of its effect on me. The earth's rotation around its axis created days and nights, and the months on the calendar kept moving, a cruel and harsh reminder that I could not stop the progress of time.

When the weather turned warm, I saw the first tiny shoots of green on the tallest branches of my frangipani tree. How had this miracle happened?

I had not watered the tree. I had not even watched it closely. Yet, the earth had revolved around the sun, the season had changed. The invisible but inevitable laws of nature had prevailed. The programming within my tree was functioning exactly as expected. Fall comes, but so does spring.

On the surface, all may seem calm, but things move forward exactly as they should, in tandem with an unseen natural rhythm.

There wasn't anything I could do but watch in amazement as the dogs barked at passing cars and the vegetable seller stopped outside my gate, his cart loaded with green mangoes, perfect for making spicy pickles in the summer heat.

Laughing

Sometimes crying or laughing are the only options left, and laughing feels better right now ~ Veronica Roth

When Amma and Dada arrived, the clouds of gloom that had engulfed me for months instantly dispersed. Although still jet-lagged from their flight, they were immediately helpful. I left for work on Monday morning, leaving Shreya in their care.

Amma's arthritis, which had begun in her knees, had now moved into her hands. Her fingers ached, especially in the mornings. She tired easily and was happy to stay home. Dada explored the neighborhood and made new friends, but they were not the same energetic parents that I remembered. I needed to hire household help to ease their days when I was at work.

While I expected to have deep conversations with them about my situation during the weekends when Shreya was away, I could see where I had inherited my sensible practicality and minimal sentimentality from. My home life hummed to a new rhythm, but it was still based on a "what now" approach instead of a "why me" litany.

We discussed the chain of events leading to my situation without drama or heated words. They knew how precarious my marital relationship had been over the years, and there was no point digging further into the mess. It was better to focus on what came next.

"What do you want to do?" Amma asked me repeatedly.

Had I made up my mind to permanently walk away from my marriage? Or was this a prolonged cooling-off measure? If I was convinced that I would not go back to that house, why did I continue to send Shreya to her father every week?

I didn't have the answers. I needed more time.

One morning before school, Shreya was in the shower while I was bustling about the house. Dada was reading the newspaper and Amma was in the kitchen. I heard a terrified scream from the bathroom that was followed by the sound of a door hastily being opened. A wet child hurtled out and into my arms, her eyes filled with fear.

The next instant, a rat scurried out at top speed from the bathroom and ran out through the main door, which had been left open for the morning breeze.

I hugged Shreya and wiped her with a towel while trying to calm her down. The rat had been sheltering in the drain and had jumped out and surprised Shreya, who was shaking with fear. Her terror was real, but at the end of the ordeal, which had lasted for exactly two minutes and didn't end badly, I wanted to laugh.

My parents were concerned about what had transpired. They'd heard Shreya scream and could only imagine what might've happened, but I relayed the details of the scene and their fear quickly turned to laugher. The adults were bursting with laughter, but Shreya was livid.

She refused to find the humor in it. Although I could not blame her—I certainly wouldn't be laughing if the beady-eyed rat emerged from the bathroom drain during my shower—I couldn't help it. I attempted to curb my giggles at least until Dada accompanied Shreya to the bus stop, a daily routine that gave him an excuse to leave the house in the morning.

As I prepared for my workday, I smiled to myself, surprised at how open I had become to all the strange things that were happening in my life.

My life still seemed like a bad dream sometimes, and I had no clarity about what I wanted in the long run, but I finally sensed a gradual return of my sense of humor. Like a curtain pulled back little by little to reveal sunny skies, each day more light penetrated the darkness that I had accepted as my destiny. The feeling felt new but also familiar.

In the most unlikely moments, I would catch glimpses of the person I used to be: the child who shrieked with delight as her dress swirled about her like a balloon, the girl who used to see the glass as half full, the young woman who used to laugh at the absurdity of life. All of those previous versions of myself had existed, yet I couldn't have imagined what the future versions would be like.

Much had happened to change my optimistic attitude to one of pessimism, but it was moments like these with Shreya and my parents that showed me who I used to be—yes, and who I could become again.

Exploring new talents

One good thing about music, when it hits you, you feel no pain
~ Bob Marley

Dada made friends easily. Whether it was at the bank when he visited each month to check his pension, the stationery store where he bought pens and pencils for Shreya, or at the local temple, he was happy to chat with any friendly face he encountered.

One day, he met Mr. Srinivasan, a retired gentleman, who lived in the neighborhood with his daughter's family. It wasn't long before Dada took Amma to their home for a visit and later returned the invitation. I was glad to see my parents settling in.

"My daughter teaches classical music, singing, to kids," Mr. Srinivasan mentioned.

"Would Shreya be interested?"

When not doing homework, Shreya preferred to read books. This had worked well for her during the months she had spent the hours after school alone at home until I returned. But now, with my parents able to keep an eye on her from the gate, she had tentatively begun to go out and make friends.

Shreya was not keen on adding other activities to her schedule, but I was eager to resume music classes. Ten years ago, after my PhD and during my infertility phase, when my life was epitomized by the Charles Dickens quote "it was the best of times, it was the worst of times," I had turned to music for distraction. Music had saved me then. Perhaps it could show me the way again.

The winter after my PhD defense, I was lost and unhappy. I had completed the last of my research work and thesis writing like a maniac, effectively blocking out the external world. I had completed all the requirements in record time, yet I felt empty.

For two years after my first-trimester miscarriage, I directed the energy of disappointment toward my doctorate. Once that lofty goal was done and dusted, I had nowhere to direct the destructive thoughts that came flooding in along with the tears.

We moved into a swanky high-rise apartment in Bethesda to be closer to his office. Our new trendy neighborhood was a stone's throw from the prestigious National Institutes of Health. The street that led from the metro station to our apartment was lined with shops and specialty grocery stores, where people conversed in unfamiliar languages as they shopped or walked purposefully toward their destinations. Everyone seemed to be enclosed in a happy bubble. Except me.

To an outsider, my life looked perfect. Yet, as the winter progressed, I preferred to stay indoors. I spent my days applying for jobs to distract myself from my doubt and despair but hardly ever received responses. When my husband returned from the office in the evenings, I would often be huddled on the sofa, teary-eyed and listless at the lack of my success—in my job search and in my marriage and quest for a baby. I cried. I hardly slept. I seldom left home.

My eyes would often be red and swollen, and the circles under them grew larger. My clothes hung loosely on my shoulders. Hollows appeared in my cheeks and there was a deep hole in my heart. I burst into tears while driving, folding laundry, or sitting by myself in the local temple. One day, I abandoned a half-filled grocery cart at Safeway, unable to contain my tears in the produce aisle.

When I received an email inviting me for a job interview with a startup located not far from home, I was excited. I ironed my formal suit, prepared my presentation, and updated my resume, still surprised by the PhD suffix to my name.

There wasn't much of a pharmaceutical industry in the Washington DC metropolitan area, so a suitable job for me would typically mean relocation, something we had not discussed. But this job description and location matched both my skillset and our preference to live in Maryland.

On the day of the interview, I showed up early at the specified address with my fingers crossed.

"Good morning," said the tall blond woman who had corresponded with me via email. She went over the day's agenda, which included an hour-long presentation to their small team followed by one-on-one meetings with key members. I nodded, eager to get on with the interview.

"Before we get started, I have been told by HR to ask whether you have a green card," she said.

"No, I don't," I replied. Before I could begin to explain to her that I had a work authorization that allowed me to take up employment in the United States, she sat up straight with a shocked expression.

"We can't go ahead with the interview then," she said, as she stood abruptly. "You have to leave now."

I looked at her, shocked.

"I don't need a green card to work..." I began again, trying to convey to her that I had valid work authorization.

She refused to listen.

"We can't interview you if you don't have a green card. You have to leave now," she repeated, moving toward me.

I stood up, confused, unsure of what I could say or do to make her change her mind. But the lady was firm. She escorted me to the front door, not allowing me to say anything further.

It was only when I drove back home did I understand that I had lost this golden job opportunity not because of any lack on my part but because of an ignorant person who was convinced that a green card was the only way a foreigner could legally work in the United States. I flung myself on the bed, crying. Could things get any worse?

As if the infertility wasn't enough of a tragedy, here was another strike against me. Both were not my fault. No matter how hard I tried, everything was stacked against me. I was cursed.

At a holiday gathering at a friend's place, I came across a reference for Nirmala Mami, a Carnatic music teacher.

"Does she teach your child?" I asked Satya, the woman who was raving about her.

"Yes. But she also teaches adults. I have been going to her for the last year," she said.

"Beginners too?" I asked.

"Yes. I started at ground zero. She is not just a good teacher, she is a wonderful person," she said.

Music had been an intrinsic part of my years growing up. From the morning chants that played on cassette tapes on the portable Panasonic player to the latest Bollywood tunes that were the rage during my college days, music was a constant backdrop of our family life. My aunts were musically inclined, if not trained, and burst into song on long train journeys or impromptu gatherings.

Amma sang devotional *bhajans* every day. She had wanted me to pursue music, but I had chosen to learn Bharatnatyam as a child, tempted by the pretty clothes and jewelry the dancers wore. Lacking the focus and stamina that dance required, I gave up a couple of years later.

Maybe it was time to dip my toes into singing.

Nirmala Mami was exactly as Satya had described. With her long braid and a big bindi on her forehead, she reminded me of a taller version of Amma. Her home, a short drive from my apartment in suburban Maryland, smelled of sandalwood incense, jasmine flowers, and camphor. The music room in the basement of her home was a temple to the arts.

On Wednesday afternoons we sat cross-legged on the carpeted floor for an hour-long class. Each class began with an invocation to Ganesha and Saraswati. For those hours, I tried to follow Mami's cues. She was methodical, patient, and forgiving.

On festive days, she would offer me *prasad* from the pooja she had performed. On other days, we would make small talk for a few minutes about live music concerts happening in the Washington metropolitan area.

I looked forward to our weekly meetings. The class taught me how to let my sadness flow through me as musical notes, some tentative, others strong. For an hour each week, I was able to dispel the melancholy in the presence of a motherly figure who didn't care about the labels that I had attached to myself—scientist, childless, depressed.

In my first year with Mami, I experienced a second miscarriage and six months of treatment for infertility that involved painful, invasive investigations that left me depleted.

I informed Mami that I had landed a coveted job in California. A few weeks later, the reproductive endocrinologist confirmed that I was pregnant.

Mami was among the first people to whom I disclosed the miraculous news.

"I am worried about starting a new job and moving to a new place. I hope everything will be fine this time," I confided tearfully as I took my leave.

"Don't worry. God will watch over you," she said, handing me a bowl of sweet *payasam* she had made that day. I bent down to touch her feet and seek her blessings.

"Practice your music, it will always help you," she said. I nodded.

I had not kept my promise. Caught in a work-home-baby cycle, I had no time to sit and sing. The cassette tapes with recordings of our practice sessions and the music sheets full of notations for the songs that Mami had neatly transcribed in her clear handwriting lay in a box alongside my maternity clothes at the top of a closet in California until I brought them back to India.

One Saturday morning, I went to meet Jaya, Srinivasan Uncle's daughter, to inquire about a one-on-one class. Although her house was the same shape and size as mine, Jaya's home buzzed with laughter and music. Most of Jaya's music students were children under the age of fifteen. Although I needed to start all over again, I was too self-conscious to join a group of giggling kids.

Unlike the calm and controlled environment of Mami's basement, Jaya's home was flooded with sunshine. From the upstairs bedroom where she taught, I could hear the television in her living room downstairs, the annoying "Jingle Bells" tune of cars reversing in the street, and the metallic clang of dishes being washed in the kitchen.

I refreshed myself on some of the compositions I had learned earlier, picked up a few bhajans, and agreed to participate in a group performance at the Ganesh festival later in the year.

When I was attending class in Mami's basement, I had felt as if my life had hit rock bottom. I had not seen any light even in the distant future because I did not have the one thing I wanted: a baby. But now, as I repeated the words to the same song that I had learned with Mami yet at a different place and time, I realized that it was possible to hit rock bottom more than once.

I had a child but not the loving home that I had envisioned.

Life was incomprehensible. I could no longer say with certainty that one event, one person, or one place would make me happy.

Countless Bollywood movies contain a severely flawed cliché: "God, please give me this, I will never ask you for anything else again."

Humans were wired to always seek more, look for the next thing, aspire for the unattainable.

I wanted peace. But peace could not be found in any object or accomplishment.

All I could do was pursue something that connected me with something outside myself, even if only for a moment. For that moment, it held my fears at bay and with each passing day, helped me climb up from the dark pit that had once seemed bottomless.

Small wins

*The more you praise and celebrate your life,
the more there is in life to celebrate ~ Oprah Winfrey*

Like many of her friends, Shreya admired Sania Mirza, a rising tennis sensation. Her success story as a local girl who had made it to the big leagues was a matter of pride to everyone who called Hyderabad home.

With her sporty ponytail, wide smile, and trademark nose ring, Sania's face was featured on billboards all over the city. She was a good role model for young women all over India, moving the focus away from movies and fashion to sport and endurance.

I was not surprised when Shreya expressed interest in dressing up as Sania Mirza for the fancy dress competition at the annual Ganesh pooja celebrations in our neighborhood. It wasn't difficult to comb her hair into a high ponytail and find a skirt and t-shirt that looked suitable for tennis, but the nose ring was not so easy to find.

It took a few days of inspired shopping to find a clip-on ring that fit Shreya's tiny nose.

Shreya was pleased with her outfit and practiced hitting imaginary tennis balls with a racket borrowed from Kiran's son who lived next door and often came over to play.

Shreya's enthusiasm was rewarded with a second prize. Kiran's sons won the first prize as superhero brothers with their matching Superman and Spiderman costumes. It was time to celebrate this unexpected win!

As we tucked into Domino's pizza and admired the tacky medals that the kids proudly wore around their necks, I allowed myself to feel that all was well with the world.

"How come you have so many books at home?" I asked Kiran, whose older son was always reading, even while walking to the bus stop in the mornings.

"Oh, I know a guy," Kiran replied with a mysterious smile.

"What guy?" I asked.

"There's a guy who has a warehouse full of secondhand books in Mehdipatnam. He sells them at a discount. Actually, I buy them by the box. He also takes them back and lets me exchange them when the boys are done reading."

"That sounds like a great deal," I said. Not having access to books was making me grumpy.

"Can you take us with you the next time you go there?" I asked.

"Of course," she said.

A few weeks later, Shreya and I piled into Kiran's car and rode up to a dark and dusty warehouse that housed thousands of books. Boxes and piles of hardcovers and paperbacks, comics, and magazines lay strewn across every square inch of space.

The children ran around crazily, amassing book towers with their selections. Shreya picked up the whole series of *Babysitters Club* along with children's books by Gerald Durrell and Enid Blyton—books that I had grown up with. Kiran's kids knew the drill and chose comics and *Goosebumps* books.

Many of the books were old and yellowed, but they were reasonably priced and certainly of readable quality. And the prospect of exchanging them was a deal I could not refuse. We returned home with two full boxes.

As the days wore on, I could sense my parents' restlessness. My life had been eased by their presence, but theirs had been curtailed. Summer in Hyderabad was brutal, with temperatures climbing upward of 40 degrees Celsius on many days. While I enjoyed office air conditioning on weekdays, the house got unbearably hot.

I bought a couple of portable air coolers that could be wheeled around to blow humidified cool air wherever we were seated. It gave us some respite, but the appliance needed to be manually filled with buckets of water, a job that Shreya was happy to take on.

As April turned to May and inched toward June with no sign of the monsoons, I noticed Shreya and my parents snapping at each other. The heat and the pressure to stay indoors for long hours was getting to them.

When I received my bonus check, I was pleasantly surprised. My team had done exceedingly well, and our reward was certainly well-deserved.

"Why don't we go on a holiday?" I asked at dinnertime.

"Where can we go? Every place in India is hot as hell," Amma said.

Amma and Dada had taken us on many holidays when we were children: trips to Kanyakumari in the south and to the cold hill station of Darjeeling in the east, pilgrimages all over the country, and a trip to the Kashmir valley to see its unforgettable beauty. We had seen the length and breadth of the country.

Those travels had not been easy. Train bookings had to be done manually in those days, and Amma had often stood in a line for hours to get our tickets. Hotel reservations had required months of planning and advance booking. Yet, they had done it.

Things were much easier now.

"How about Goa?" I asked. Despite its proximity to Mumbai, we had never been to India's prime tourist destination.

I had seen an advertisement for an all-inclusive hotel package at the Taj Holiday Village resort in north Goa, which offered complimentary airport pickup and drop-off. Indigo Air had recently announced a direct flight from Hyderabad.

"What will we do in Goa?" Amma asked.

"Stay in air-conditioned comfort in a five-star hotel for a few days, watch the sunset, and relax," I replied.

"That will be too expensive," Dada said, though his ears perked up when I mentioned the Taj hotel.

"I think it's OK. We all need a break," I said, brooking no further arguments.

With a phone call to inquire about a suite and a few clicks on the airline and hotel sites, we were all set for our four-day getaway. I had taken my parents to Disneyworld and Niagara Falls on their visits to the United States, but I had not made all the bookings.

Whenever I'd visited India during those years, my parents had made all the arrangements for domestic travels. This was the first time I had taken charge of holiday bookings.

In Goa, we took a half-day bus excursion to the city, but mostly we lolled around in the room all day watching movies on the big-screen television. We stepped out for lavish breakfast and lunch buffets each day, and Shreya played in the sand and swam in the pool. I read books on the verandah of our quaint bungalow that faced the ocean. Every evening, we went for a sunset walk on the beach.

Nothing changed on my personal front, but there was a peaceful cadence to those few unstructured days and nights.

It felt important to acknowledge our small successes, to stop and observe the tiny pockets of sunshine that broke up the boredom of our monochrome days and made us smile.

I didn't know then, but that was the last holiday that Shreya and I would take with both of my parents.

Celebrating a birthday

Ultimately, it's the simple things that make a difference
~ Chris Smalling

"What will we do for my birthday?" asked Shreya.

Like all children, her immediate concerns revolved around her own life, even though her life was quite different from those of her friends.

Shreya's calm acceptance of the new normal—weekdays with me and weekends with her father—had been a welcome surprise. A small part of me had expected her to make a fuss about moving between homes. She often forgot her books or shoes and became anxious, but she quickly learned to plan ahead to ensure she had everything she needed on Friday mornings, since she went straight from school to her father's house.

Even more surprising, and inspiring, was the open way in which she talked about it with her friends. Without even a tiny bit of self-consciousness, she would say "I am at my Dad's house this weekend." It had pinched me a bit when I heard it the first time, but I quickly recognized the wisdom in her direct approach.

No one questioned her about the reason for this unusual living arrangement. Frankly, it was none of their business, but on a more pragmatic level, you couldn't expect an eight-year-old to go into the details of their parents' split. I envied her easy confidence.

"What do you want to do?" I asked.

I had never been a fan of huge birthday celebrations, both for the expense and the work involved in organizing food and games for little kids. The whole system of receiving redundant gifts and handing out return gifts made me squirm. But Shreya was turning nine and was expecting some acknowledgement of her special day.

We shopped for new clothes and bought chocolates that she would distribute to her friends and teachers in school, an annual ritual that she looked forward to.

"I don't know. Something?"

A clear ask is easy to fulfil, but an ambiguous one is much more difficult.

What could I organize on short notice?

Back in California, I used to take a day off from work so that we could simply hang out. I had taken her to a petting zoo once, and to a park where she fed ducks and ran around the lake chasing bubbles. I might have carried on the tradition each year, but Shreya was a conscientious child who enjoyed going to school, especially on her birthday. She didn't have to wear her uniform that day and enjoyed her short-lived popularity thanks to the bags of candy she handed out.

I sent her off to school, still unsure of what to do later that evening. I left the office earlier than usual and stopped by Country Oven, her favorite store for snacks and pastries. I picked up a choclate cake customized with a birthday message and bought some samosas and curry puffs.

Dada bought her favorite Lays Magic Masala chips and Coke from the small store in our neighborhood.

Shreya returned from school pleased with the day's events. She had handed out every single chocolate and emptied the bag in the school bus on the way back. I went to the bus stop to pick her up, an unusual surprise for her since I was never home at that hour. I smiled at her enthusiasm. We had talked about ordering pizza that night and she was looking forward to it.

"What is this?" Shreya exclaimed when she entered the house and spotted the unusual collection of goodies on the dining table.

"Did you bring cake? And chips? And Coke?" Her eyes widened first with surprise and then with genuine delight.

"Yes. Let's have a party," I said.

"But who will come?" she asked.

"Call your friends, the kids who play with you every day," I said.

It was an impromptu party of the best kind. An hour later, half a dozen sweaty, hungry kids entered our home. Radha brought her children over, a surprise for Shreya, who was thrilled to see their familiar faces. All the kids sang the birthday song and clapped as Shreya cut the cake. I handed out plates piled with slices of cake and chips. No physical gifts were given or received but there were smiles all around.

"Thank you, Amma," Shreya hugged me when her friends left. "It was the best birthday. Ever."

I thought back to Shreya's first birthday party at a hotel in Hyderabad, an event that her paternal grandparents had organized. Shreya's fifth birthday in California had been a casual pool party where her friends munched on cake and Cheetos and watermelon slices after swimming in the condo pool.

There would be other birthdays, with or without parties. One day she would turn sixteen and then twenty-one, and cross other milestones that would not be purely age related, but also achievement related. We would come across other crossroads in our lives, but it felt good to pause and celebrate the ordinary things that made up our days.

Working with my strengths

What makes you different or weird, that's your strength
~ Meryl Streep

"I am thinking of signing up for a certification exam," I told my parents on a Monday morning before leaving for work.

On weekends, I spent time with them, trying extra hard to make sure they were comfortable. By leaving their familiar life in Mumbai, they had done me a huge favor. I was grateful.

After decades of family responsibilities, their retired life had been an easy one. I knew Amma loved the phase of her life where she did not have to participate in or witness the busy life of parents with young children. When she came to California to help me at the time of Shreya's birth, she had made her stance clear.

"I raised my children. Now it's your turn," she said, when I returned to work eight weeks after giving birth.

She may have wished for me to stay home and enjoy motherhood as she had, but I was committed to my career.

"If you are in a desperate situation, I will come and help you, but on a daily basis, you need to figure out your life," she said.

Her words seemed a bit harsh and out of place, but I could not argue. She had put her life on hold for the first five months of Shreya's life. Her presence had given me enough time to settle into motherhood and to make alternate arrangements for Shreya's care.

Although Amma and Dada had visited me in the United States a few times after Shreya's birth, it had been more of a long holiday for them. They would take turns spending time with me and my younger brother, who lived close by. We would take them on short sight-seeing trips and indulge their small requests, but most importantly, we spent time with them.

The "desperate situation" that Amma had made an exception for but that I had never envisaged arrived when I walked away from my husband's house, not in the United States but in India.

Amma was back in a home with a working daughter and school-age granddaughter, forced to participate in the daily details of my buzzing home. I felt guilty. Once again, I reached out to Kumari, my neighbor from across the street, to help me find a suitable cook.

Fortunately, I was able to hire a lady who came in the mornings to prepare breakfast and lunch, freeing Amma from the burden of kitchen duties. Occasionally, I would ask Raju the driver to come on Saturdays so we could visit the Birla temple or spend time by the Hussain Sagar Lake. Sometimes we ventured out to music concerts.

I made it a point to avoid discussions regarding the fate of my marriage with my parents. Like a cat that closes its eyes while drinking milk, I proceeded through the days and pretended there was no problem.

But there was a problem: I was not ready to formally file for divorce, but I was not comfortable in this holding pattern either.

The day-to-day firefighting that I had been managing single-handedly until my parents' arrival was no longer necessary. I felt supported. I had more bandwidth. I needed a goal, something tangible to apply myself toward. When an opportunity to upgrade myself at work arrived, I decided to take it.

Adding the burden of studying for a certification examination to an already stressful situation may sound like an excessively foolish idea, but what can I say? Learning is part of who I am, so I could not resist the opportunity to undertake a new challenge.

I had six months to prepare for the four-hour online exam. If I succeeded, I would obtain a credential that would add credibility to my experience and give me visibility as an expert in my field. Who knew how this might come in handy in the future?

I expected my parents to protest. My life trajectory had changed wildly from anything they (or I) had expected. They could have pointed out all the other things I needed to reprioritize. But, to my surprise and eternal gratitude, they did not.

While I looked at the successful outcome as a way to salvage some part of my life, Amma understood that the process of moving toward the goal itself would save me.

"How do you plan to do it?" Amma asked.

"Just like I did back in my school days. Wake up early every day and study for an hour. I hope that will be enough," I said. I braced myself for their objections, but there were none.

Amma knew that I loved to learn but that I also loved to win. I had never failed a formal examination.

If I failed this time, would it make me feel worse at a time when I was already feeling low? Whether she considered these doubts or not, she chose to keep them to herself.

And just like that, I became a child again. A child who loved school, studies, and even exams.

I woke up at 5 a.m. and sat at the dining table with my books and pens: reading, taking notes, memorizing details that would be required for the exam. I had to make the most of the quiet early hour to concentrate on the task at hand. It was a gift of time that I gave to myself, to engage myself in a way that made me feel alive.

Never a night owl, always a lark, I had always studied early in the morning in Mumbai. During my PhD days, I managed to get everything done at the university between 9 a.m. and 5.30 p.m., and at my job, I made it a point to never bring work home. Now, for this certification, I didn't want my studying to interrupt the flow of normal life.

I didn't need permission from my husband to do this. I didn't have to face his objections or obstruction. It was a relief to be able to pursue a goal without having to apologize for my interest or ambition. Was the exam an attempt to delay discussions of the inevitable? Perhaps. But I didn't care. Every day I used my power of concentration, indulged my pleasure in lifelong learning, and kept up my hope that this credential would further bolster my expertise. Stepping into each day with this focus turned my attitude from despair to anticipation.

What my parents knew and I didn't (at the time) was that this simple step of parking my attention on something constructive and using my strengths would build my self-esteem.

Instead of considering myself to be a failure, I could see myself as a success, even if in only a small way.

Happy place

When in doubt, go to the library
~ J. K. Rowling

In my childhood, books had been my avenue of escape and adventure. Although the school library had left much to be desired and formal libraries weren't common, the streets of Mumbai had yielded many treasures on its roadside markets and hole-in-the-wall shops that doubled as lending libraries.

In the United States, I had devoured the content in the local libraries, but returning to India had taken away the simple joy that I derived from having access to more books than I could ever read.

I had signed up for a membership at the British Council library in Hyderabad within the first month of our arrival, but I gave up after a year thanks to the distant location, outdated collection, and the inconvenience of borrowing and returning books.

I didn't mind the austere look of my sparsely furnished house, a deliberate decision to keep things simple during this time of transition, but I missed having books around. On my frequent business travels, I picked up books at airport bookstores, justifying the purchases as a necessity. Although I had enjoyed Paulo Coelho's *Alchemist*, I had been disappointed in his subsequent books. Towering displays of Chetan Bhagat's books were hard to avoid, and many new voices introduced by the Indian publishing industry made me despair about falling literary standards.

Eager to make my home a reflection of my taste, I embraced the impulse to buy when it came to books, yet I avoided adding mediocre books to my personal collection. I wanted to sample a variety of books—classics and contemporary reads, fiction and nonfiction—without having to allocate a permanent spot for them within my home.

How lovely it would be to have a local library, a place within walking distance with a modest but growing collection, I mused one night, knowing that such a wish was highly unlikely to come true.

Yet, sometimes, the benevolent librarian in the universe is listening.

Evening Hour, a brand new library, opened not far from my home. The founder, Priyanka, was an enterprising young woman who had returned from the United States. Spurred by the lack of library access for her own children, she had decided to take action. She envisioned her fledgling library as a social space that would be more than a mere collection of physical books.

The first time I entered Evening Hour, I saw a large room in a commercial property partially filled with shelves and books. A secluded room offered a separate space for author meetups and children's activity sessions. Shreya was happy to see all the children's books. I enrolled as a member, and Priyanka and I instantly became friends.

When I told Priyanka about my forays in writing, she asked me if I could write book reviews for Evening Hour.

Since the column *"Round Trip"* that I had written for *India Currents,* I had stopped writing altogether. The upheavals of the past year had taken a toll. My words had dried up even as my emotions had run unchecked. I did need an outlet for all that I was feeling but was reluctant to share the confusion and misery that was woven into every aspect of my life.

Even as I became more comfortable with my single-parent lifestyle, there was a feeling that my gains were built on the ruins of a broken marriage. It seemed dishonest to write about the small things in my life that made me smile without tackling the elephant in the room.

Priyanka's suggestions to write book reviews for her blog was exactly the impetus I needed. It gave me a reason to visit her warm book-filled library often. It offered me a reason to read widely as well as deeply, and it gave me an outlet for my writing.

I discovered a wide variety of books by Indian authors: *The Music Room* by Namita Devidayal, a memoir that doubled up as a beautifully narrated primer about Indian classical music; thought-provoking titles like *Custody* by Manju Kapur; and sweet novels like *A Girl Like Me* by Swati Kaushal that reflected my current status.

Interspersed with these were humorous books, insipid books, disappointing books by famous authors, and a handful of books that should never have seen the light of day. I discovered old classics, new authors, and unexpected gems by well-known or barely known writers. Most of all, just being in a bookish place made me happy.

Sharing my love for reading with a kindred soul who had set out to make a difference by investing in an enterprise made me admire Priyanka and compelled me to support her in any way I could. Later, I would write about Evening Hour on my blog, which would include book reviews and a plug for Priyanka's enterprise.

On International Women's Day, I invited a handful of my friends to watch the movie adaption of *Eat, Pray, Love* in the private viewing room at Evening Hour, a cozy space with a comfortable red sofa and overstuffed chairs. We ordered samosas and chai and chatted for a while after the movie. It was a welcome break for everyone, but more importantly, an opportunity for us to make time in our lives for ourselves.

Nourishment comes in many forms. So does happiness.

Surrounded by books and friends, sharing food and stories, I felt content. Somewhere deep in my soul, a palpable ease settled in. Yes, there was a part inside me that was broken, but the edges were not so jagged anymore.

The sharp tips of sadness that used to pierce me at all times of day and night in the early months of separation, which had morphed into a constant dull ache, had now become a rare occurrence.

There were days when I did not feel any pain. Perhaps there was a scar that would always mark the wound, a reminder of what had changed, but it did not stop me from moving, growing, and becoming more of myself.

Free from the constraints and contortions that married life had demanded of me, I was now uncoiling, shrugging off the restraints forced by society and my own limited beliefs.

Many years ago in Napa Valley, I had observed a hot air balloon laid out on an open field in the pale predawn light in preparation for inflation.

With every burst of the hot flame, its hollow core expanded, and a gigantic colorful sheath came to life. It righted itself without support and rose upward—pure physics and pure beauty.

Nature's laws did not discriminate. With the correct inputs, there was only one way. Not only did the balloon stand tall but it grew strong enough to carry a basket with people in it, up and above the verdant vineyards. The view from above was breathtaking, but the view from the ground was no less.

Finding my happy place and surrounding myself with the people and things that nourished me moved me towards wholeness. There was no doubt. Perhaps, with time, I would rise and float above the petty mess of ordinary life—and maybe even become strong enough to carry others along.

A beginning had been made.

I was ready.

Writing my way out

The aim of art is to represent not the outward appearance of things, but their inward significance ~ Aristotle

Always a reader, never a writer—that's how I saw myself.

Having a stack of books within easy reach made me happy. Evening Hour satisfied my urge to check out new books every week. For a brief while before leaving California, my writing for *India Currents* had brought me solace and some success.

From a short story that won a small award to an early essay about identity that made its way into a college-level English composition textbook, I had been pleasantly surprised by the unexpected reach of my words.

During the second trimester of my pregnancy, I began penning my thoughts into a Word document on the home computer. A couple times a week, I would take a few minutes to write about my pregnancy, a common universal experience that most women share but one that had eluded me for so long.

I hoped it would grow to be a long letter to my child, a collection of my trivial thoughts and grand ambitions, but more importantly a record of my child's early years.

The small wish to document my state of mind at an important phase of my life turned me from a reader into a writer. From pregnancy woes to delivery room drama, I began writing about Shreya's growth and development, detailing the many firsts of a baby's life but also those of mine as a new mother.

I wrote about her toothless smiles and silly babble, sleep habits, and food preferences. I wrote at night after she went to bed. The days were long and tiring, but I loved that precious sliver of solitude when I could express my gratitude for a life that included a child. The alchemy of writing transformed my overwhelm and exhaustion into something that I valued. I became aware of a creative force that gave me clarity and renewed vigor to face the next day.

At some point, my writing morphed from a self-centered act of documenting my child's progress to a rumination of what it meant to be a woman who had a career and ambitions beyond the remit of wife and mother. When Shreya fell sick, as all kids in day care do, I wrote about working mother guilt.

If I traveled for business, I felt an acute need to overcompensate for my absence with gifts, a phenomenon that I had condescendingly dismissed when I observed it in others—before Shreya entered my life. There was always more on my plate than I could manage, yet writing did not feel like an extra burden. Paradoxically, it made my load lighter.

The monthly column I had written about returning to India had been my last piece of writing to appear in print. The part of my brain that had found solace in writing long essays filled with insights seemed to have regressed or disappeared altogether.

"Why don't you write a blog?" a friend suggested.

"What is a blog?" I asked

"You go online, open a free account, and begin writing. It's like an online journal," she said.

My first thought, uncharitable as it was, was that blogging seemed like a self-serving navel-gaze in the public domain. Why would anyone want to read an individual's ramblings?

But I was wrong. Blogs were at the leading edge of a rapidly changing cultural phenomenon. Facebook would soon spur a social media epidemic by providing a forum that allowed one to parade their private life (or at least the most glamorous parts of it) before an eager audience.

I was not ready to write something that others could read. I had stopped the pregnancy/baby journal when Shreya turned two. The plan was to print it, bind it with a pretty cover into a nostalgic keepsake and give it to her on her sixteenth birthday, a day that was so far away in the future that I could not yet envision it.

Yet, the memory of writing it made me smile. My writing time had been my personal oasis. A small respite each night, a private space to muse and vent. It was a restorative act, not a performative one.

Should I begin writing a journal again?

I had read somewhere that the act of expressive writing, including journaling, can help deal with trauma and that spending a few minutes each day to write down your thoughts can have a therapeutic effect. Even for nonwriters, transforming experiences into words can be an instrument for healing.

I didn't know all that as I considered starting a new journal (in addition to the gratitude journal in which I jotted bullet points), but I knew that writing was my preferred way of making sense of my world.

When I asked Shreya if she had a spare notebook, she handed me a plain ruled notebook from her stash of school supplies. Like I had done a decade ago, I chose the hour before bedtime to spill my thoughts into receptive pages that did not judge my words, my grammar, or my thoughts.

It should have been easy. After all, I had done it before. But the baby journal project had been a celebration of life, a triumphant outpouring of gratitude for my good luck in having struck the jackpot of motherhood, something I had strived and wished for. Now it was the opposite.

All that came out was a litany of complaints, a stream of rage and resentment at the unfairness of life. What could I achieve by pouring poison into the unsuspecting pages?

I wrote anyway.

I asked the pages, "Why me?" The question came up repeatedly. The answer was not simple. The world was unfair. Everyone had a better/easier/happier life.

Who put me in this position? It felt good to blame others. My parents were responsible for insisting on my marriage even though I had not been ready. Shreya's father was impossible to live with. His family had never accepted me. Society would not give us a break.

Why did I not learn how to deal with these situations? When I exhausted the list of others to blame, I turned the finger to myself. Guilt had the answers. I must have done something wrong. If only I had fit into the mold of a traditional housewife, if only I had been able to cook better, my life would be different.

The more I wrote, the deeper I spiraled into self-pity. One night while rereading my ramblings, I noticed that the story I had written about my life read like a stereotypical Bollywood movie script from the sixties and seventies.

A hapless woman with no independent means, typically a mother, whose life was nothing but a mountain of woes brought about by her own bad luck.

The image made me laugh.

I certainly was NOT that woman.

Even as a child, I had scoffed at the portrayal of such women in popular movies, asking my mother why the woman didn't escape from her abusive family or find a way to support herself. While it was true that I was going through a tough phase of life, there was much that also felt right. Why else would I feel so light?

Writing rescued me again. This time by showing me the error (and humor) of seeing my life as a series of unfortunate events.

I would go through this sequence repeatedly. Periods of intense doubt and self-pity in which I would wallow without remorse. I let myself feel it deeply, without trying to reason with it. Like a virus infection that wipes you out for a couple of days, I allowed it to wash over me completely. And, at the end of forty-eight hours, I would walk away from it.

Forty-eight hours of self-pity became my new mantra.

I let myself shout. I punched cushions like a boxer in training. I welcomed the suffering. I let myself cry.

And then, when the storm of self-pity had passed, I would shake hands with it and see it off like a friend who had come for a short visit.

The journal was proof of my process, a catalyst for transformation and a witness to my metamorphosis.

Be a part of something larger

Strive not to be a success, but rather to be of value
~ Albert Einstein

My workplace was located on a beautiful green site at the intersection of a busy highway and the entrance to a large industrial zone. In contrast to the noise and pollution caused by incessant traffic on a road that was in various stages of disrepair across the seasons, the campus was a green oasis.

Once inside the gates, lush tropical trees lined both sides of the blacktop road, and grape vines languidly creeped up on supports as the road made a sharp turn to the building where I worked.

The laboratories on two floors of the hexagonal building that resembled the shape of a benzene ring had large windows that overlooked a well-maintained lawn with a variety of shrubs and bushes. My days at work were spent learning, listening, and contributing to a cause that was close to my heart: discovering new medicines for unmet medical needs.

Over and above the practical considerations of making a living, I considered my chosen career as a blessing because, at the heart of it, it helped people lead healthier lives.

There were surprising perks of working in India. The canteen served freshly cooked Indian meals, offering a variety of vegetarian choices. An office assistant, Sitaram, cleaned my cabin, made photocopies, and fetched multiple cups of coffee and tea on demand.

The downside, of course, was the tendency of people to probe into your personal life.

"What does your husband do? How many children do you have? Where are you from?"

Although I shared my troubles with a few colleagues, it was like a tap I could open and close at will. I missed the privacy of life in the United States where people seldom asked nosy questions.

The other part of my American work life that I missed sorely was access to reliable day care. Back in California, Catherine, a licensed day care practitioner, had cared for Shreya from the time she was five months old like a benevolent and watchful grandmother. I had learned much from her.

But most importantly, Catherine's attention to the children in her care had allowed parents like me to focus on their work.

In India, organized day care, particularly for small children, was nonexistent. Most families with infants and children below school age cobbled together a system that involved grandparents, unskilled part-time or full-time helpers, and local preschools. My workplace employed many highly educated young women who suffered due to lack of family support and good-quality day care options.

Unlike other office-based jobs that can be done from home, a career in science involves spending hours in the laboratory and performing experiments that do not always conform to a predictable nine-to-five schedule.

Offering an on-site day care facility like many companies in the United States did would certainly help not just young families (particularly mothers, who tended to drop out of the workforce after giving birth) but also the company, who would directly benefit from better retention of skilled employees.

Radha and I talked about this over a cup of tea one afternoon. Could we float the idea of a day care to our management? Even though Shreya spent most of her days in school, I still worried about her long-term after-school care. The problem was eased by my parents' presence, but I knew it would not last forever.

Radha had a complicated system of paid help to watch her kids and relied on her mother's support very often, and we knew that junior staff with infants had a much harder time finding affordable childcare.

An informal survey showed that there would be great support for such an initiative. We co-opted another colleague who had also worked in the United States and had seen firsthand how his wife, who was equally qualified, had chosen to stay home for the sake of their child. He felt equally strongly about our cause.

We formed an ad hoc task force to look into the practicalities of introducing such a benefit. We split the task load, which involved interviewing potential providers who were willing to set up a facility in the industrial area in which our office was located, visiting prospective sites, and figuring out the exact combination of services, hours of operation, and details that would be specific to our work life at the company.

From making PowerPoint presentations to compiling spreadsheets to track enrollment and calculating the breakeven point, we went from scientists to marketing and finance professionals. The greatest hurdle was convincing human resources, the department in charge of staff welfare, of the business upside to our proposition.

From concerns about liability by locating it on-site, fears that employees would interrupt their work to visit their children during work hours, to brushing off the whole premise as a trivial issue, every imaginable hurdle and objection was hurled at us.

"We haven't heard about such a request in any of our other units. I agree that the research arm has more women employees. This seems to be a women's problem," the head of human resources said after hearing us out, without studying the in-depth scenarios and numbers that we had worked out.

Huh?

Was he implying that women were having babies on their own? Was childcare (and not just childbirth) only a woman's lookout? And were the contributions of women employees not significant enough to warrant consideration of their personal lives?

The hard-to-swallow truth is that employers want only those parts of employees that are of use to them. Like a selective organ transplant, they are keen to preserve only those aspects that maximize output without considering the ecosystem that makes every employee perform optimally. Addressing the hygiene factors that improve focus, concentration, and therefore productivity is a longer but more profitable game. These issues just need to be seen through a human lens instead of a purely business one.

The human resources head was not keen on the initiative even though all the details had been figured out. We had identified an interested provider, shortlisted a suitable property just outside our gate, and lined up a roster of parents who were eager to enroll their children.

We had negotiated and arranged for a separate area where children as young as three months could be cared for in order to cater to those women who had to return to work at the end of maternity leave. The day care staff was trained to cook and provide fresh, wholesome meals to children and engage them with toys and activities. All we needed was an initial startup grant to cover the costs of retrofitting the existing house to make it childproof.

Radha and I were disappointed not just at the lack of support but from the lack of vision. How could a management representative be so clueless about the daily dilemmas and difficulties that young women faced everyday as they chose to come to work, jeopardizing their physical and mental health and the well-being of their children? The amount of money in question was large but not prohibitive, certainly a drop in the bucket for the organisation.

Companies routinely spent much larger sums on advertising budgets and corporate social responsibility initiatives, all of which are prominently featured in the in-house and mainstream media as a brand-building activity. Yet when it came to making a real difference to the employees themselves, they shied away from taking a bold stance.

We regrouped and discussed options, convinced that we were on the right track. Whether it benefited the organization or not, it would certainly lift the burden from our beleaguered colleagues who were short of options.

Should the three of us pitch in with our own contributions to jump-start the initiative?

Should we approach a nonprofit or philanthropic organization to help us get started? The final decision was left to the head of our research unit to decide whether he wanted to deploy part of the discretionary benevolent fund toward this initiative. We made one last pitch to our local management.

Was it our impassioned championing? Was it our persistence? Was it just a way to get rid of us? I cannot tell, but one day we received a check for the startup amount that we had requested.

The day care, aptly named Sunshine, began operations within a month. We had predicted a breakeven point somewhere in an eighteen-month time frame, assuming a full occupancy within a year. To our delight, we were at full capacity within four months and Sunshine became profitable well before the end of the year.

Shreya spent her summer holidays at Sunshine. She hung out with Radha's kids and also made new friends. Because it was located right across from the office, parents could spend more time with their children, both while dropping them off and picking them up, using the commute time to bond.

Years after I left the company, I would hear that the success of our "first-of-its-kind" day care initiative was not just embraced and brought on-site but replicated at the other units. I felt a pinch of anger at how the idea, which had once been callously dismissed, was being claimed as their own. There had been no public or private acknowledgement of our efforts.

Yet there was no doubt in my mind that our work had been visionary and essential. Even though it helped others, it helped me more. Being a part of an initiative to solve a problem of this proportion gave me a purpose that was much larger than my own.

Getting away from it all

*One's destination is never a place but rather
a new way of looking at things ~ Henry Miller*

There were days when I wished I could escape my life. Every day, no matter how productive or ordinary, was still a reminder of all that was different from the life I had imagined.

Returning to India was supposed to be a grand homecoming. Instead, I was once again renting a home, much like we did in the years in the United States when we had changed addresses frequently.

I craved stability, the safe zone of a home that was loving and unchanging, like my parents' home had been and still was. They had lived in the same tiny apartment where I had entered as a baby and left as a bride. My permanent address was a fixed one. Its coordinates were etched into my memory in the same way that the walls of that home were marked with my scribbles and laughter. After sixteen years of marriage, I had wanted the same kind of stability for Shreya in India.

How could I have known that life would turn out this way?

Amma and Dada had dropped their plans and moved in to help me, but they had created a routine in their golden years that was suited to their stage of life. Even though I mourned the end of my "normal" life, I could not stop them from living theirs.

They preferred to spend their time attending devotional music concerts and lectures on the Bhagavad Gita. There were weddings they wanted to attend and pilgrimages they hoped to undertake.

"Go," I said, when Amma asked me gently if they could travel for a few days. My tone and expression contrasted with my words. I was surprised and angry and afraid. How would I manage without them? I took a deep breath. If it was hard for me, it must have been even more awkward for my parents to ask their daughter for permission. Everything was so messed up.

"It's just for two weeks. Shreya has holidays for most of the time. Can you manage?"

Their hesitation unnerved me. It didn't have to be like this. They didn't owe me all of their time. I was grateful for what they could spare.

"It's fine, go," I said, gently this time.

In theory, I could take a few days off from work and hang out with Shreya. Perhaps we could go somewhere.

While I was married, I had never taken the lead on the logistics of holiday planning. I was happy to simply get away and leave the details to him. Except for flights to India, I had never gone away with Shreya on a holiday.

Now, I had to figure out somewhere to go that would be safe and fun for the two of us.

"What are you doing for the school holidays?" I asked Kiran, over the wall that separated our homes.

"I'm spending a week at Rishi Valley, the residential school. They have a center where you can stay and study the teachings of Krishnamurti," she said.

I had heard about the school but didn't know much about Krishnamurti, the philosopher who had founded it. The school was located by the small town of Madanapalle, on the border of Karnataka and Andhra Pradesh.

"Why don't you and Shreya come along? I'm taking my boys. The kids can all hang out," Kiran said, opening the door to a possibility of getting away that I had not known existed.

I followed Kiran's instructions; sent emails, booked tickets on the overnight bus that would drop us off in the early hours of the morning in an unfamiliar rural neighborhood, and arranged for transportation to the school. Fortunately, all the arrangements came through smoothly, and weeks later, Shreya and I occupied a pretty cottage with a round verandah tucked away in a corner of the school campus. Kiran and her boys were next door.

Almost exactly a year after moving out of what I had hoped would be my forever home, I felt calm. The nights were eerily silent. The dark sky showcased millions of stars that were invisible in my urban neighborhood. There were no automobile sounds—even the cell phone signal was weak.

Except for mealtimes, which were strictly enforced, the children were free to run around or cycle through the campus. Kiran and I spent time in the well-stocked library with its smooth red oxide floor and large brass pots filled with fresh flowers.

With each day, I felt my breath slow down. A deep peace rose from my feet into my stiff shoulders and neck. I woke up looking forward to another calm day instead of dreading the mad rush from bed that marked the days for both Shreya and me. There was no difference between weekdays and weekends. The kids climbed the tree outside our bungalow or played board games during the afternoon. In the evening, we visited the farm where organic vegetables were grown. We often stopped by the picturesque sunset point where students and teachers meditated at twilight.

"Why don't you put Shreya in a boarding school while you figure things out?"

I don't remember who said it to me, but I do remember taking offense at the suggestion that I was unable to manage my life as a single parent.

Boarding schools were for parents who did not want to or could not participate in the daily life of their children. Whether it was the parents' peripatetic or dysfunctional life, the end result was that the parents missed the opportunity to watch their children grow up.

I was already missing large parts of Shreya's life by being away at work for long hours and because of her weekends with her father. Yet I had never considered sending her away either for her benefit or mine. We were yoked together by biology and karma. Our situation was not ideal, but at least we had each other.

The campus was remote and idyllic. A safe bubble. For a brief moment I was tempted to inquire about a teaching position. I could enroll Shreya here and teach. Instead of struggling each day to ensure her safety, we could both live here, ensconced in the large family of teachers, students, and alumni who visited frequently. I allowed myself to get carried away until I performed a reality check.

While the school was safe and serene, it was not a financially viable prospect for us. I had to ensure that I could earn enough during my working years to save for Shreya's college education and our long-term future.

Even if I pursued the inquiry with the school administration, I knew that their offered monthly salary would be insufficient for the nest egg that I needed to build. Plus, Shreya's father would probably not agree to this plan.

I gave up on the idea of moving here as a permanent option but resolved to make the most of the time we had on the beautiful campus. I soaked in the silence and the morning sunshine and noticed how completely the darkness descended soon after sunset. Birds flew freely, unfettered by electric wires and mobile towers. Even the stray dogs moved softly without displaying any aggression.

There was a reason I was here. Not just for a break from my life but for a chance to reexamine it.

What will the parents say?

Become comfortable with not knowing ~ Eckhart Tolle

Being a planner doesn't mean you can prepare for every possible scenario.

The current ease of my life was supported by my parents' willingness to temporarily live in a city that was new to them. While they realized how important it was for me to retain my job, I could tell that they were restless.

Dada was a Mumbaikar at heart. Despite the difficulties of living in a city that wasn't very kind to senior citizens, he had been reluctant to leave Mumbai after retirement. Instead, my parents had moved into a new apartment in a less crowded suburb a year before their most recent US trip. They had furnished it as per their current lifestyle and preferred their quiet life and independence.

"Why don't you move to Mumbai with us?" Amma asked.

They took turns asking me this question at least once a month. I dreaded the conversations that followed because everything they said made sense.

"You can easily find a new job there. There is a good school right across the street for Shreya. We will take care of her while you work. It is a familiar city for you. Your career prospects will be even better—think about it."

Their points were valid and their arguments sound, but there was one problem.

Moving to Mumbai meant Shreya would not see her father. Although we had been a disaster as a couple, he had always been a doting father. In California, he had often taken Shreya for rides on his bicycle, strapping her into a child seat behind him and wrapping her up in a jacket, a little red helmet on her head.

When she was three, he bought her a tiny tennis racket so that she could run around the court or hit a few balls as he played with his friends. In Hyderabad, he had fulfilled her wish for a puppy, who she named Sparky, just before our separation. He took her to malls and movies, and they bonded over Sparky on weekends.

He was the fun dad, I was the dull mom. The strict mom. The all-business mom. I knew that Shreya needed both of us because we were so different. Though her days with me were boring and predictable, she was assured of my support for school and homework and exams. Weekends with me meant tagging along on errands as I tried to catch up on everything that had accumulated during the week.

Weekends with her dad gave her a break from the seriousness of life that covered me like a mantle. I could not shake it off, but at least she could get a breather.

Given my tough road to motherhood, I considered Shreya a gift bequeathed to both of us. I could not treat her like property and use her as a bargaining chip or tool for reward or punishment while we figured out the next steps. I was clear about that.

"You still have sympathy for him even though he doesn't care about you," Amma said.

I had always considered Amma to be a reasonable person. She had brought up her three children with an unwavering sense of fairness that had had a deep influence on how I viewed life. Although she didn't say much, she saw people for what they were rather than what the gossip would have her believe.

Amma was upset with her son-in-law for what she saw as his primary failure in keeping his family safe.

Who knows what goes on in a marriage? Even my parents, who had a compatible marriage, had their points of contention. They had figured out how to disagree and how to find common ground.

Upon their arrival in Hyderabad, Dada boldly went to my in-law's home one afternoon when I was at work and confronted them. He was livid. According to his old-world approach, families were responsible for keeping marriages intact. He had fired off a series of questions, not expecting answers or any resolution. He wanted to vent and he did not mince his words:

"How could you allow this to happen? They lived in your house.

How can you sleep soundly knowing that your daughter-in-law and granddaughter are living alone in some corner of this city?

Do you not have any shame?"

Amma too was angry but had no intention to see the people who she considered responsible for turning a blind eye.

"I gave my daughter, a string of pearls, to a bunch of monkeys," she said, surprising me with her choice of words given her general reticence.

"When I die, I don't want him to come anywhere near my dead body," she declared one day. Her uncharacteristic declaration, more in line with Bollywood melodrama than a reflection of her personality, was a clear indication of her distress at my situation.

In the months they spent with me, I went through several rounds of such conversations.

"Once you take the bold step of leaving your home, your marriage is like broken glass. No matter how much you try to fix it, it will be like putting plaster on a gaping wound," Amma said.

While I understood their concerns—and even agreed with them in some ways—I refused to use Shreya as a pawn against her father.

For the time being, I had a good job, a supportive boss, and some measure of stability—and I could breathe again. What I needed to learn next was how to live with the ambiguity of the future. I had to decide how to release my parents to get on with their lives while I also got on with mine, with or without their reassuring presence.

Growing up is never easy. We think it happens when you reach a certain age, accomplish a goal, acquire a house, or reach a milestone, but it doesn't stop.

When in the presence of my parents, I often allowed myself to feel like a child. Yet when I saw my parents and my child tugging me in different directions, I had to do the grown-up thing; I had to learn to let go.

I was not prepared to separate Shreya from her dad. It wasn't fair to her even if moving to Mumbai would be easier on me.

There was only one thing I could do.

"You go back to Mumbai," I said. "I will manage."

Forgiveness

Without transcendence, life has no beauty ~ Deepak Chopra

The thing about marriages, bad ones especially, is the utter disregard with which the couple and those around them treat the cracks when they first emerge. Like tectonic plates that crush and grind against each other under the surface of the earth, the damage does not happen on one sunny morning when the earthquake hits. When a couple splits, it is the result of an inevitable break that has been brewing for years without respite.

Unlike the earth's geology, which is more or less impossible to adjust, human relationships can be tended to and rebuilt, strengthened with attention and support, but the mending often takes more resources than what family and society are able to provide.

What do you do when you know that staying together is not easy and breaking up is even more difficult?

In the two years following my departure from my husband's home, I found ways to work around the common factors that deter many women—money, safety, security, social stigma.

Yet, a part of me wondered whether I had done right by Shreya. She was, after all, the apple of her father's eye, and mine too. We both loved her desperately, a fact that I mentioned to Shreya repeatedly, always stating that she was a very lucky girl. She had two loving homes that she could claim. But had I stolen her opportunity to have a normal childhood, one where both parents lived under the same roof? Would she be labeled as a child from a "broken home"?

In putting my safety and comfort ahead of her long-term well-being, was I being selfish?

In the months after my parents left, Shreya's father was cooperative. He was happy to have her on weekends and when I traveled. Although we spoke only through messages relayed through Shreya, there seemed to be a different kind of cadence to our always-fiery interactions when we had lived together. I even joked that the secret to getting your spouse to cooperate was to separate.

My first employer in California offered a generous employee assistance program that included a few free confidential sessions of counseling for employees who needed help with family issues. Even before Shreya's birth, we had met a couple's counselor who, although unfamiliar with the system of arranged marriage that had yoked us together, explained the basics of communication in a relationship.

During Shreya's toddler years, life became extremely hectic for me. Managing home and work and a young child had taken a toll. A different counselor reminded me that expecting my spouse to read my mind was not a realistic or helpful coping strategy.

I would have to figure out a practical way to ensure my needs were met. If I needed help, I would have to speak up and ask for it as well as make other arrangements to ease my load.

Hiring a cleaning lady to put the house in order every two weeks, rescheduling my yoga classes, and requesting him to occasionally take Shreya for her swim lessons had worked. For a while.

Yet, we soon slipped into past patterns of behavior where our unspoken unhappiness spoke volumes about our marriage.

Friends and relatives had tried to intervene, but everyone was biased, inclined to take sides and argue for whoever they felt had been wronged. Their good intentions were clear but so was their lack of skill in tackling our long-festering problems. I needed someone attuned to the cultural nuances of marital relationships in India, someone trained to help couples like us but sufficiently detached.

Although I had been to counseling several times in the United States, I had not sought advice from a couples counselor in Hyderabad. While I knew I had done the right thing for me by walking out of my dysfunctional marital home, I wanted some assurance that I was not taking an irreversible step if there was a slim chance that our relationship was salvageable.

It wasn't easy to locate such help. Online resources were next to negligible. I didn't know anyone who had been through (or admitted to) marital counseling. I would have to disclose some details to others in order to look for options. When a colleague suggested Seva, a nonprofit that offered free marital counseling, I decided to give it a try.

The center was located in a dilapidated building with high ceilings, a relic from the Nizam era.

It took me two hours to get to the center, but I spent every Sunday morning with Sunil, the kind counselor. For an hour and a half, Sunil asked questions and listened patiently to my long responses.

I explained not just the situation but also my reasons for my decision, my disappointment, and most importantly, my expectations for a reasonably happy (yet not perfect) married life. Surely, sixteen years together should have molded us into some version of compatibility that we could both accept?

Sunil asked pertinent questions.

Did moving back to India and living with in-laws trigger the situation? What did I see as our temperamental differences? What were my value systems and life goals? Did I think it was the family's (and society's) expectation that a woman's place was in the home responsible for this situation? Was my professional success a barrier to intimacy and acceptance?

We reasoned out several scenarios, most of which pointed to extrinsic circumstances as possible causes for the fallout and not basic incompatibility.

Sunil met separately with Shreya's dad on Wednesday evenings. After months of discussion, Sunil recommended a temporary reconciliation.

"Why don't you try to live under one roof again? This time on your terms," he suggested.

"Despite how far you have come, you have a seed of doubt whether you have done the right thing for your child. Both of you are very focused on your daughter. Why don't you begin seeing each other again? Plan occasional outings as a family first. Then try to make it work by staying together for six months. If things change, that's good. If not, you will have the satisfaction of knowing that you did the right thing. Only then will you be able to move on. You deserve to be happy."

I respected Sunil and agreed to his suggestion.

One Sunday evening, we decided to meet for a movie, *Mr. Bean's Holiday,* as a family. The plan was to meet at the theatre and Shreya would return home with me. I reached PVR Cinema on time, but in my hurry to get there, I forgot my mobile phone at home.

When Shreya did not arrive even after the movie started, I went in, angry with myself for trusting that he would keep his word. I figured that he would make some excuse and relay it through Shreya. I was livid at his callousness.

When they finally arrived, we sat through Mr. Bean's funny antics with hardly a smile. The tension between us was at a breaking point. There was no question of having dinner together. He offered to drop us at home. I sat with my lips tightly pursed in the front while Shreya reclined sleepily in the back.

"How could you forget your phone?" he hissed.

"It's not a crime," I replied. "Why were you late?"

"We left on time. There was an accident and a traffic jam," he said.

I accepted in his explanation, knowing that it was probably true. Traffic in Hyderabad could be unpredictable. We sat in silence for a while.

"Everyone thinks it's my fault. Everything is my fault, even when there is a reason that's beyond me," he said.

I looked at his profile, his face looking straight ahead as we waited for the traffic light. A soft halo enveloped his features in the mellow light of the evening. His posture expressed defeat, a helplessness that tugged at my heart.

A wave of compassion flooded over me, washing away not just the anger of the evening but also the rancor of our years together. We had endured health issues, infertility, job loss, and major moves together. We had a history that was complex and messy and invisible to anyone else.

The years together did count, if only for the fact that we had both grown up together, not as siblings do in childhood but as young adults married at an age where we didn't know each other but also didn't know ourselves. Our prejudices and passions, our biases and quirks, our ambitions and weaknesses had projected themselves in every situation that had demanded kindness and understanding from each other.

We were both at fault. Who was I to claim the high road?

Later, I would consider those few minutes in the car at twilight at a nondescript intersection as a "moment."

In her memoir *Seeking Peace*, Mary Pipher describes moments as "discrete time, complete in themselves and utterly distinct from the habit-bound wave time in which we all live much of our lives. While minutes are earthbound and can be measured, moments both merge with eternal time and exist outside time altogether."

In that moment, I dissolved into eternity, a feeling that was both intense and fleeting. I floated above myself while still remaining connected to the bones and skin that made up my body. All of my thoughts and emotions felt petty and trivial in the grand cosmic plan that encompassed me.

Why not try once again to make it work? I returned to reality convinced that we needed to reconcile. Sunil had suggested six months, which sounded like a reasonable length of time to set us straight.

He moved in with Shreya and me. My parents were not pleased but remained tight-lipped. If they had doubts about the success of this experiment, they didn't mention it.

After all, like me, they were practical people. They could have questioned my naive optimism, but they couldn't fault my pragmatism.

I had to figure out my life given its constraints, including the limited support they could offer.

No more doubts

*Don't spend time beating on a wall,
hoping to transform it into a door ~ Coco Chanel*

The road to hell is paved with good intentions, it is said, and I couldn't agree more.

Seven months after we began our experiment in living together, Amma died of sudden cardiac arrest on a Sunday morning. We left Shreya with his parents and took the first flight to Mumbai.

As we waited in the airport, weighed down by grief, I wondered if I was doing the right thing. In an uncharacteristic fit of anger, Amma had declared that she didn't want her son-in-law around when she died. Was I disrespecting her by letting him accompany me to the funeral?

No one is prepared for the death of a parent, regardless of their age, health, or circumstances. Despite knowing that in the natural order of things your parents will leave the world before you, when death actually strikes, it can evoke many feelings beyond just grief.

What could I do? Everyone seemed relieved that I had put the blip of separation behind me, assuming it was a trough in a rocky marriage, a midlife aberration that had sorted itself.

Amma had not been happy with my decision. She felt let down. By capitulating to him, she felt I had lost all the ground I had gained by separating and setting up an independent functional household. She didn't say all this, but I could feel it in her stoic silence.

Although Amma looked like a traditional housewife of her generation, she had radical thoughts that she didn't often express.

I recalled a conversation with Amma when I narrated an experience with a doctor during a medical examination required for my green card application. It occurred during the phase of infertility treatment when my arms would often be bruised and blue from multiple blood draws. The doctor performing the examination asked me about them.

"I'm trying to have a baby," I said.

"You have a PhD and a job you love. Why are you so keen on having a baby? Is all this not enough? Why are you spending your retirement money on trying to have a child?"

"In my culture, children ARE the retirement plan," I had replied impertinently.

When Amma heard this, she said, "The doctor was right. Do you really need to go through all this to have a baby?"

I was taken aback. On my behalf, Amma had endured sly questions and innuendos that there was something wrong with me for not producing a child seven years after marriage. She knew the expectations of the society we inhabited.

But she also knew the status of my marital relationship and how that skewed everything.

What others didn't know was that Amma was an only child, born to an incompatible couple. Although both her parents loved her, she could see how harmful their relationship was to each other, and how it contributed to the general home environment of her growing years.

She knew firsthand that the common adage "once you have a baby, all will be well" was not true. Given that my married life was not smooth even before the arrival of a baby, Amma could foresee the difficult road that lay ahead once a baby arrived, both for me and for the baby. I was oblivious to her concerns.

"You don't know how it feels. You had three children without even thinking about it," I had replied, hurt that she didn't understand my anguish.

My drive to procreate was not in response to the "when will we hear the good news?" type of questions from well-meaning friends and relatives. My longing was rooted in biology, hidden in a place where logic could not enter. I wanted a child, so I could be a mother, like her.

I had seen the close bond she shared with her own mother, the friendship they shared, over and above their genetic connection. I wanted that.

My logical mind, my preferred way of understanding the world, could go only so far in trying to rationalize this irrational desire. The emotional side of me wanted to experience the feelings that overwhelm women during pregnancy and childbirth and in rearing children. The inexplicable concoction of hormones and happiness that was eluding me was the one thing I craved above all else.

The tension in my marriage was inconsequential, or so I thought.

When Shreya was born, Amma shed tears as she held my hand in the delivery room, pleased with the successful outcome of "project pregnancy" but apprehensive about my future.

Amma had been right. Our daughter had been a boon and a distraction for our marriage. She had helped us grow individually but had not helped us bond. In fact, things had gotten much worse for us as a couple.

In our last face-to-face conversation two months ago, Amma asked again what I intended to do about my marriage. She knew about the reconciliation experiment, which had extended beyond the originally agreed upon six-month period. Yet, in her usual sensible manner, she weighed it against all she had seen and heard in the last eighteen years.

"Are you planning to continue like this?" she asked. I didn't have a firm answer.

"My mother was not educated. She had no money and no choice. She was forced to stay in her marriage. I had two parents who loved me, but they were not meant to be together. All three of us would have been much better off if things had been different, if my mother had been given a choice."

"But aren't marriages made in heaven?" I countered, taking a dig at her for having arranged mine.

"Sometimes even God makes mistakes. Half a century ago, my mother suffered. Today you are suffering," she returned.

"But you are educated, financially independent, and emotionally strong. You have worked hard, and you have been bold enough to walk out. You CAN make a different choice. If you choose to stay—for the sake of society, for the sake of the child, or for any other reason, and remain miserable, what use is all this empowerment?"

Was Amma really pushing me toward divorce? She didn't say the words outright, but then that was never her style. Her questions always got to the heart of the matter. She was showing me the way but letting me choose. Amma could be so maddening sometimes. Particularly when she was right.

I looked out the window of the aircraft as it moved swiftly toward Mumbai, unwilling to believe that I would not see Amma alive ever again. My tears fell in an unstoppable cascade. Amma had been right. The experiment was not going well.

Despite my best intentions following the moment of transcendence that I had experienced in the car after the movie, living together had once again activated our past behavior patterns. I was conscious of my triggers and tried to avoid them. I stayed away from his parents and avoided asking questions about his work or health.

But we were two doomed characters in a dystopian universe, repeating the same mistakes within the walls of our home. There were no loud arguments, but I was always on guard. The cadence of life changed. My previously peaceful home was now back on high alert.

I had worried about Shreya being labeled by society as a product of a broken home, but all I was doing was making her a spectator to our miserable marriage, just like Amma had been to her parents' marriage. Is it better to grow up in two separate but peaceful homes or in one that is outwardly cohesive but inwardly dysfunctional?

While Amma's childhood home was not literally split into two parts, it had been broken in spirit. Yet Amma had turned out okay. Better than okay, actually, with her education, her sense of justice, and her unique way of seeing the world. She had been a major force in my life, one whom I loved and trusted unconditionally. She had raised her three children to be productive adults, capable and caring, concerned about their lives and of those around them.

I thought of all the years and discussions with Amma in which she had tried to make me see my situation differently. She had been a front-row spectator, first as a child and now as a parent of someone who was in a bad marriage. For all my talk of emancipation, I had fallen into the trap of caring deeply about "what will people say," having internalized the cultural taboo of divorce.

I would never be able to consult Amma again. I would have to figure out the next steps on my own.

Two months after returning from Amma's funeral, my well-intentioned experiment blew up. On the parched ground of my grief and anger at Amma's sudden death, when familiar frictions emerged, the sparks grew into an inferno and burned all of my remaining doubts about divorce to ashes.

Choosing to surrender

Try something different—surrender ~ Rumi

I thought about that six-week workshop about divorce that I had attended years ago in Palo Alto. We were now in round two of our separation, but this time there was no going back. No more counseling, no more dithering.

Shreya had once again adjusted to the split-home situation without much of a fuss. She knew the drill—weekdays with me, weekends with her father.

Even with our currently strained situation, he was still the fun dad. On weekends, they would take Sparky for walks around the park, get something to eat, and later head out for a movie.

He didn't have to rush her to school each morning or worry about her safety or homework when she returned. As always, I continued to shoulder more than my share of the hard work of parenting.

I had to seriously consider my prospects if I formally filed for a divorce. There was one big reason for my procrastination, something I had not shared with anyone.

A few days before walking out of my marriage, I had visited a lady lawyer at her home office one evening to find out how the courts in India decided about custody.

"In case the couple cannot choose for themselves, even for a child as young as eight, the court will ask the child who she wants to stay with," she said.

"But I am the more responsible parent," I replied.

"Even then. The child's wishes will be taken into consideration," she replied.

I mulled over her words. Even though my life was becomingly increasingly unbearable, I knew that if Shreya was asked for her preferred parent, she would pick her dad. After all I had undergone to bring her into the world, the thought that she would choose him made me ill. But she was just a child.

Torn between my sanity and my love for my child, I had left my husband's house but kept my child with me. I didn't mind sharing her, but I didn't want to lose her.

That single session with the lawyer almost three years before had convinced me that I could carry on with this charade of separation forever.

Shreya was the lottery that we had both won. The wish that had come true, at least for me. In her I saw the embodiment of the cliched warning: be careful what you wish for because it may come true.

My wholehearted wish on the hot summer day in Rameshwaram for a child of my own had been granted and this perfect little girl had brought joy and purpose to my life. She had also made my connection with her father irreversible, if not unbreakable. But I refused to think of her as my property or use her in a custody battle.

After our two rounds of separation, if Shreya was asked now, would she choose to stay with her father?

I didn't know the answer to that. My guilt and insecurity kept me awake at night. I had prolonged our separation phase because I did not want to put myself in a situation where I would have to find out. I preferred to remain in this state of limbo where I could have my child with me, even if it was only on weekdays. It was not fair. Nothing was fair.

But I knew that I could not continue this charade anymore.

In the parable where King Solomon has to decide which of the two women who claim to be the mother of an infant is telling the truth, he suggests the unthinkable: cut the child in half. The woman who wants to be proven right agrees to the solution, whereas the child's real mother agrees to part with her child in order to save its life.

I thought of this woman one evening when Shreya returned from her father's home, relaying excited stories of the things they had done on the weekend. Her face radiated joy. Clearly, she enjoyed being with him, and I knew that he was a different person with her.

While we each seemed to bring out the worst parts in the other, Shreya brought forth the most loving and tender aspects of her father. Even as I despaired over the tension between us, I could not turn a blind eye to the fact that Shreya was happy in his company.

What would happen if she chose to live with him? I asked myself.

The answer was loud and clear: she would be valued, prioritized, and loved.

As her mother, what did I want for my child? I wanted Shreya to be happy.

Could she be happy outside my daily, direct control? The answer was yes.

It was a blow to my ego, but it was true.

The epiphany lifted a great weight off my shoulders. Even though I could not understand the grand scheme of things, I could see what was truly important when I applied a simple filter—my child's well-being—to the situation.

Instead of an ego-based fight with our child at the center of the ring, I could put her on a safe pedestal and take her out of any unpleasant negotiation.

During the peak of my infertility journey, I had arrived at the simple conclusion that if motherhood was not in my future, I would work toward finding out the mission for my life.

I understood now that my child was an instrument for my growth, regardless of whether she lived with me or with her father. I would have to file for divorce not knowing how the child's custody would play out in court. But I was finally okay with it.

It felt like surrender, but it was a victory. I had reached a new milestone in my mothering journey.

IV

RECONFIGURING LIFE

One small change

*We must be willing to let go of the life we've planned,
so as to have the life that is waiting for us ~ Joseph Campbell*

In the scientific community that I inhabited, many companies espoused a "fail fast" philosophy. In order to conserve resources or direct them to projects that are most likely to succeed, nonviable projects were terminated as quickly as possible. To ensure that decisions were based on facts, as scientists we were often asked to design a "killer experiment"—one that could unambiguously prove or disprove the hypothesis.

Our six-month "live together again" plan had been that killer experiment for our marriage. Sunil had been right; I was able to come to a clear conclusion. Our dynamic was toxic. It could not be fixed by moments of transcendence or truckloads of good intention. We could not live together. Not for society, not for our child, and certainly not for each other.

If I felt that I was not seen or acknowledged or supported by my husband, I am sure he felt the same way about me.

Each of us felt hollow and insignificant to the other. Enveloped in our own misery, we had neither the bandwidth nor the willingness to help each other grow. In fact, with all the water under the bridge, we had reached a point of no return where everyone who had written me off as being stubborn or stupid for taking the step of walking out of my marriage was now convinced that it was for the best.

Most importantly, I harbored no more doubts.

I was forty years old. My mother was dead. My marriage was over.

Our big house became peaceful once again. With grief as the backdrop, the incessant rhythm of my work life sustained my life financially but wore me out on a daily basis.

Late evening calls, monthly presentations, quarterly meetings, deadlines, managerial issues—the list was long and exhausting. For each crisis that I could anticipate or avert, a million minor mishaps waited in the wings.

Shreya was a responsible child. She opened the door to the house with her key, fixed herself a snack, and watched TV for a while before tackling her homework. By the time I returned, she would be ready to go out and play. At 4 p.m. on weekdays, I would step out from meetings to call home to check on Shreya and remind her to not open the door to anyone.

I avoided late evening calls and declined invitations for company-wide events where booze and conversations flowed freely and were followed by dinner at luxury hotels. Many of my colleagues looked forward to these networking events where they could posture and present themselves for promotions and pay raises, but I had different priorities.

Over the years, I had watched in astonishment as many of my peers ascended the corporate ladder with dizzying speed. I felt cheated, not just personally but for all women because the cards are stacked so unfairly against anyone who seeks balance between their personal and professional lives.

One evening I received a call from Kumari.

"Hello. Just wanted to let you know that Shreya is with me. Don't worry," she said.

"Why? Did the maid not come?"

"Yes. Shreya waited at the bus stop for a while then walked home. You had told her not to enter the house alone, so she came here. I have given her something to eat. She is doing her homework," Kumari assured me.

My heart sank. Shreya had walked home alone from the bus stop. She had followed my instructions, but I knew that she would be uncomfortable at Kumari's home. I returned home as quickly as I could.

I needed a regular income to support the two of us, there was no doubt about that. Yet, what could be more important than Shreya's safety? Without the presence of a reliable person, preferably a family member who was devoted to Shreya, I could not do justice to my job. My new life and current job were not compatible.

There was another thing though, which had more to do with me than with Shreya. Always exhausted and worried, I was not in the best frame of mind when I returned home. I snapped at Shreya for trivial things.

I barely listened to her. I flitted from one thing on my to-do list to the next. My scattered attention and low reserves of patience and energy made it impossible for me to enjoy my time with her.

Not only was I being unfair to her, but I was also cheating myself of the joy of raising my child. Everything felt heavy and burdensome.

I had to figure out a way to earn money without going to the office. Was that even possible?

The aftermath of a disaster brings a special kind of clarity about what is important and what is truly valuable. My fortieth birthday had been a turning point in how I saw my life. Instead of seeing it as a pinnacle that must be climbed via the vertical career ladder that was placed in front of me, jostling and pushing others and using skills that didn't always make me happy, I began to see it as a mountain that I could choose to scale at my pace.

I could walk the gently sloping wide road around it. Or I could take a break and watch the view. I could choose the narrow path that was not well marked but seemed interesting, or I could create a new path for myself. The time had come for me to break from convention in more than one way.

On a slow weekend, I sat with a pen and notebook. I listed all my monthly expenses: rent, utility bills, food, salary for the maid and Raju the driver, plus gasoline, travel, and discretionary spending. Shreya's dad paid her tuition fees, but I wanted to ensure I could cover that in case he changed his mind at any time. I needed to earn enough to cover these recurring expenses and maybe a bit more to add to my savings.

I looked at my bank account that received the monthly influx of my salary plus the associated trading account, which held the stock grants that I had been awarded. I had no idea how to sell or buy shares. Like the gold jewelry my parents gave me at my wedding, which rested in a safe deposit locker, the shares sat in their dematerialized form, like an IOU with no tangible benefit.

The amount I had paid the builder three years ago, hoping to have my own apartment, was stuck. The land on which he was planning to build was mired in litigation over property rights. I had the option to pull out the money or leave it there until the matter was resolved. The builder was a reputed one, not likely to declare bankruptcy and disappear overnight. Although it seemed like a bad investment, I decided to leave it there, not sure if it would ever convert into a stable roof over my head.

Yet, I was pleased to see that I had accumulated a decent amount of savings since the time I had begun to manage my own money. I had never really been without a monthly source of income since leaving my father's home. But in all the years of working in the United States, I had not claimed ownership of the rewards for my labor. The money in this salary account was solely mine, proof of my sustained efforts at work. It felt good to see that something of my new life had grown even though so much of my past had exploded into nothing.

Since leaving my husband's home, I had earned well and spent wisely. I had set up a sparsely furnished but comfortable home that was my refuge and my sanctuary. The only way I could manage my concerns about Shreya's security was to figure out a way to work from home. My job did not allow such an option, which meant I would have to resign.

The benefits of working for a reputed company far exceeded the salary, designation, and recognizable logo on my business card. Quitting would mean letting go of the car and the driver, a convenience that I took for granted. The annual bonus, health insurance, and future stock options would all go away as well as my prospects for promotion and further advancement.

Turning my attention back to the list of monthly expenses, I struck off those that would be unnecessary if I stayed home: petrol, salary for Raju, and the cook, who had continued after my parents' departure. In a separate column, I added new ones. I would need to buy a personal laptop and perhaps a Blackberry, but these would be one-time expenses. On a recurring basis, I would need to allocate money for local transport.

I had to ensure that I could earn a minimum amount each month without having to dip into my hard-earned savings.

"Why don't you move to the Mumbai house with me?" Dada suggested one day. We were suffering in similar ways, I thought. He was a widower and I would soon be legally divorced. Both of us were mourning the end of a long relationship.

Amma's death had forced Dada to leave his beloved Mumbai. Although he loved his children and grandchildren and took turns staying with each of us, he yearned to go back to Mumbai every few months and stay in his own home.

His visits to Hyderabad cheered me up. It felt good to have another adult at home. He would walk Shreya to the school bus each morning and bring her home in the afternoon. But I knew how restless he got after a few weeks. I did not want to make him feel obliged to stay with me for the long term. He had spent a big chunk of his life's savings on my wedding all those years ago. Not having any idea of how ugly or drawn out the divorce would be, I wanted to save him from the trauma of watching me wade into the murky waters of court proceedings to dissolve my marriage.

I mulled over Dada's suggestion once again. The Mumbai apartment was fully operational, and I could get a new job without too much trouble. Living in a rent-free house in my home city would further reduce the financial pressure. When both Amma and Dada made the same suggestion a year prior to her death, I had resisted them for a variety of reasons.

Nothing much had changed. Actually, things had gotten worse. Back then, I had been concerned about disrupting Shreya's already fractured life and separating Shreya from her father. Now, I needed to stay in Hyderabad until the legal aspects were sorted out.

I could not handle a big move at this time. All I needed was to make one small change that would fundamentally change my life.

What I needed was a way to work from home, preferably during the hours Shreya was at school. It was time to reinvent my work and my life yet again.

Collaborate and create

Kindness is like snow - it beautifies everything it covers
~ Kahlil Gibran

In Louise Hay's book *You Can Heal Your Life,* which became my bedside best friend, I once again came across the practice of gratitude as a life-changing tool. Although I had made a habit of regularly writing down the things I was grateful for, particularly on difficult days, I had not considered using it as a tool to tackle a big task such as a job change. Louise claimed that a consistent gratitude practice could be applied to any aspect of your life that you wish to change—money, relationships, home. If you want to change your job, be grateful for the one you have, she advised.

I was grateful for my job, but the sense of satisfaction I had previously experienced had diminished. Some of it was extrinsic; supportive bosses and colleagues had quit, management policies had changed, and on a daily basis I no longer felt the thrill of going to work.

Many hours were spent in unnecessary meetings, resolving interpersonal conflicts among staff, and writing reports. The days were long and unproductive. I was convinced that if I could work alone I could produce the same output in half the time.

What could I change about my current job?

Working from home, even for a few hours a day, was not endorsed by company policy. Could I negotiate for a part-time arrangement? I had experimented with it before in the United States when Shreya was a toddler. After great deliberation, I had negotiated a four-day workweek in order to have a spare day to spend time with Shreya and to catch up on household chores.

What I did instead was work extra hard on the days I was at the office to complete all my assigned tasks, partly in gratitude for the option and partly to ensure I was not seen as a slacker. After a year of giving 100% and earning only 80% of my salary, I felt exhausted and cheated. I vowed never to do it again, so I only briefly considered this option before dropping it.

Should I move to a new company? Jobs were plentiful in Hyderabad. The city was booming and the pharmaceutical industry was thriving, yet I was hesitant to exchange one employer for another and walk into a job where I would have to prove myself all over again. Everything seemed possible but nothing seemed practical.

Psyching myself to feel grateful for my job in its current state was not easy. Although I thought of myself as a skeptic, I knew that faith was a powerful force. I had seen it work for others and also for me. The success of Louise Hay's book and, more importantly, her personal story convinced me to try the approach.

As I entered my office each morning, I silently blessed everything in it. I wordlessly thanked my employer, my colleagues, and even my email inbox. I blessed my desk and chair in the corner office that I occupied, the beautiful green campus in which I spent my days and expressed gratitude for the job that sustained me financially.

I looked for the small joys at my workplace, including the casual conversations with the young women who worked in the laboratories, the comfort of an air conditioned office that helped me survive the unbearable summer heat of Hyderabad, and the pleasure of talking to Sitaram, the office assistant who was thrilled to practice his English with me when he brought me coffee. There was much to be thankful for, I quickly realized.

At a conference in Mumbai, I met Shirin, a lady who had quit her job with a large multinational corporation to do freelance work.

"There is a lot happening these days. Many foreign companies are looking to outsource work to India but need some kind of independent evaluation and ongoing supervision. I provide that for my niche since I have worked in the industry for over fifteen years," she explained.

My expertise was in a different area, but the principles remained true. Like her, I had both experience and contacts in the United States who could be potential clients. Keen to test the waters by reviving my connections, I joined LinkedIn.

When I mentioned this discussion to a former colleague, he immediately introduced me to Anu, another dynamic entrepreneur who had quit her well-paying job to start a consulting business. Over long telephone calls, Anu shared her experience.

"Don't expect to make the same money as your current salary each month, it can go up or down. Building a client base takes time," she warned. "Have an idea when you step out but be prepared to tweak your vision and your approach. Consider if you are willing to sacrifice the benefits of your cushy corporate job. You will have to do every single thing yourself, at least in the beginning."

Her words inspired me but also made me aware of the pitfalls of such a change. My middle-class upbringing had conditioned me to believe that having a salaried job at a reputable organization was the pinnacle of professional achievement. The security of a regular paycheck was the bedrock of my current life. Was I ready to embrace the erratic nature of such an enterprise?

I was not, yet I had to do it.

When I informed my colleagues about my plans to resign, they were surprised, yet I felt a sense of relief. The ones who knew about my personal situation wondered if I was being foolish by giving up my only source of income. Others thought I was throwing away my promising career for some frivolous pursuit or a life of leisure, assuming I was married and supported by a rich husband. But it didn't matter what others thought. To me it felt right.

During the notice period, it felt odd to show up at work without feeling any long-term commitment. I just had to get through the day. I did not have to think about future improvements or career development plans for either myself or for my staff.

"Love your work, not your job," some wise person had advised me long ago.

I did love the work and the meaning it held for me beyond the obvious financial security it provided. But the job required more than what I was willing to offer. I was looking forward to putting my time to better use than attending inefficient meetings, preparing endless presentations, and having difficult conversations about appraisals and bonuses. There was no doubt in my mind that the productive part of my workday was less than half the time I spent on site.

What would I do with all the extra hours in my day? Hours over which I would have complete control? The mere thought made me giddy. More time would directly translate to a better quality of life.

Yet a part of me knew there were things I would miss, like the separation between home and work, the exchange of ideas with coworkers, the opportunity to meet new people, and the leverage offered by being part of a large company.

I would miss my colleagues, wise seniors whom I looked up to, interesting peers who challenged me, and wide-eyed juniors who approached me for mentorship.

I would also miss Sitaram, who had greatly improved his command over English by taking the initiative to learn to read and write the alphabet since I had met him. By practicing with me, his spoken English had improved, but he confessed that he didn't feel confident speaking to anyone else in the office.

"Do you want to continue to learn to speak English?" I asked.

"Yes, madam," he replied with a shy smile.

"Are you ready to go to an institute to learn?" I asked.

"What time, madam? I am working till 6 o'clock," he said.

"Let me check," I said.

On the fourth floor of an unremarkable building near my home was an institute that claimed to teach "spoken English." It wasn't uncommon to see such training centers all over Hyderabad.

From answering phone calls to processing transactions, India was slowly turning itself into the back office to the world, and every city was vying for business.

During my last week at the office, I took Sitaram to the center and introduced him to the senior teacher. I explained Sitaram's situation and his interest in learning. The teacher looked surprised but didn't express his doubts. He estimated that a six-month course would be sufficient based on Sitaram's existing level. I paid the fees, making Sitaram promise to learn as sincerely in this environment as he had done at work. I had no doubt he would.

Shirin called one day to alert me to a project that was perfect for me. I would have to first send a proposal for the scope of work specified, and if chosen, I would need to spend two days in Mumbai to complete the work and write a report. I had no idea how to write a proposal or create an invoice, but the women who had guided me thus far helped me with the nuts and bolts of being a solopreneur. I landed my first project as an independent consultant. Louise Hay's method had worked!

My new work life was not without its associated difficulties. On a month-to-month basis, I made less money but gained the flexibility I desperately needed to make time for Shreya and also for Dada who often came to visit.

The loss of a fancy designation on a well-known company's business card was offset by my ability to handle unexpected school holidays and Dada's medical check-ups on short notice.

Over time, I worked with Shirin, though more often with Anu, with whom I began to brainstorm ideas and grow our reach as a team.

We created joint training programs, collaborated on projects, and offered our complementary services to prospective clients. We looked out for each other, were gracious with introductions, and generous with recommendations. I blessed every potential lead and every person who served as a resource or offered a testimonial.

Soon, Mondays became my favorite day of the week. I woke up eager to check my email and see if any unexpected leads had materialized over the weekend. No commute. No politics. No gossip. I could not remember the last time I had been so excited to get to work.

However, being self-employed took away one boss and replaced it with many; current and prospective clients who expected a prompt response. As founder-director of my one-person organization, I was queen and drone, boss and peon. I had to play all instruments and ensure everything operated like clockwork and sounded like music.

Giving back

If you want to lift yourself up, lift up someone else
~ Booker T. Washington

The freelance work ebbed and flowed as expected. In the first few months, I focused on reaching out to old colleagues from my US days and new acquaintances made in India. I requested introductory emails and references. I printed business cards with my name on it, without the logo or superstructure of the publicly traded company on which I had previously leaned. My professional life was now as adrift as my personal life had been when I had dissociated from the security offered by the institution of marriage.

"What work do you do, Amma?" asked Lakshmi, the maid. Since I worked from home, she was the only other person I saw during the hours Shreya was in school. She had seen housewives and women who went to the office to work, but I was the odd one who claimed to work, even though I was always home. She appreciated the flexibility it offered her since she could come and go as she wished to sweep and mop the house, but that didn't quell her curiosity.

"You won't understand," I said, laughing. "But I work, just like you work here."

When she was unwell or away, she sent her younger daughter in her place.

"Why are you not in school?" I asked the young girl when she first showed up.

"I don't like school," the girl replied, tossing her thick braid across her shoulder and picking up the broom.

"My Akka (elder sister) likes school. So, I help my mother," she replied.

I was curious. What exactly did the elder sister do? How much older was she? How had she managed to avoid being drafted into the same labor cycle? I asked Lakshmi.

"Jyothi thinks she is too smart for this work. She has finished tenth class," Lakshmi said, not pleased.

"What does she want to do?" I asked.

"I don't know. She sits at home, waiting for something to happen." Lakshmi's exasperation was clear. I asked her to bring Jyothi to meet me.

The next day, a neatly dressed young woman showed up at my doorstep with a folder in her hands.

"I am Jyothi, Lakshmi's daughter," she introduced herself.

I asked her in and went through her folder. It had a copy of her resume which listed her school qualifications and other details. Her tenth-standard board exams transcript showed a decent score. Although her face was too serious for a girl of her age, she had a steely demeanor that I could not ignore—she believed that she could do better than her mother, but she didn't have any practical skills to land her a job.

My former employer had a corporate social responsibility initiative that provided vocational training to young people to enable them to earn a livelihood by leveraging their limited education. I reached out to former colleagues to find out more.

I took Jyothi with me to the center located a few kilometers away. Jyothi would have to show up six days a week for a twelve-week course that would refresh her basic language and math skills and provide practical training to prepare her for a variety of entry-level jobs. Most importantly, the organization would help her find a suitable job.

"Are you ready?" I asked Jyothi, who seemed a bit overwhelmed by the neat classrooms filled with young students who looked like her. The center bristled with an energy that was contagious. I was prepared to pay for her training, but I needed her commitment.

She nodded. On the way home, I reiterated to her the necessity of completing the training. It was her best shot at landing a job and convincing her mother that her education and training had value. To my surprise, the training program was free. However, there was an expense associated with getting to the training center for three months. I gave Jyothi the money for bus fare, knowing that Lakshmi would consider the expense to be wasteful.

In the weeks following this outing, I was often tempted to ask Lakshmi how her daughter was faring. I also wondered how Sitaram was doing at his English-speaking course. Although I was curious, I didn't want either Sitaram or Jyothi to feel that they owed me anything, not even an update.

For some reason, our paths had crossed. At that intersection, I had been the instrument through which an opportunity had been handed to them. What they made of it was their responsibility.

Whether they squandered it or exchanged it for a better life had nothing to do with me and everything to do with them.

During my first semester at the University of Maryland at Baltimore, I noticed that the professors didn't mark attendance. Students walked in and out of classes as they pleased. I had been shocked at the casual nature of the teacher-student dynamic, which was so different from what I had been used to in India. One day I asked Dr. A why he didn't insist on students showing up on time for his classes.

"We are here to provide an education," he started. "I already know the stuff I'm teaching, but the students don't. If they show up, they learn. If they don't, it's their loss, not mine."

I had marveled at the sense of detachment, a sentiment that I had not seen in the first two decades of my life in India. A large part of my childhood had been about doing things because it was expected, not because I wanted to do it. From being on my best behavior to please parents to being diligent at school to impress teachers, life had been a series of keeping up appearances. It had never been about what I would learn or miss if I didn't take responsibility for those blessings that had come into my life.

That single conversation with Dr. A had changed my outlook on life. Every time I came across an opportunity that seemed interesting, I embraced it wholeheartedly because it was for my benefit or learning and not for showing off or impressing others.

Jyothi and Sitaram were on their own journeys. It was their lookout now. My part was done.

A year later, I would run into Jyothi at my neighborhood sweet shop, a popular chain that had many branches all over the city.

With gloved hands, she would weigh out the sweets and smile at me shyly from behind the counter as she handed me the box.

And many years later, when I met Sitaram again, he would proudly show me photos of his wife and children and explain, in English, how he had progressed at work.

Each time I would be reminded of the "Do It Anyway" prayer inscribed in Mother Teresa's home in Kolkata. The concluding words—*"In the final analysis it is between you and God. It was never between you and them anyway"*— were not just wise words but practical ones to live by.

My professor had taught me by example how he lived by those words. Jyothi and Sitaram had given me a chance to do the same. How could I not be grateful?

Creating connections

The authentic self is the soul made visible
~ Sarah Ban Breathnach

The new terminal of the Mumbai airport was deserted on a Sunday afternoon. My flight to Hyderabad was not until 7.30 p.m., so I bought a book at the airport bookstore and settled myself in a seat that was furthest away from a noisy construction zone.

Visits to Mumbai made me sad. Not long ago, I would have happily booked tickets to Mumbai, knowing I would see my parents, spend some time at home, and stop pretending to be a grown-up for a short while.

I loved the vibe of big cities. After Mumbai, New York and London were my two favorite cities in the world. After Amma's death, Dada had decided to close the house and split his time between his three children, shuttling between Kolkata, Bangalore, and Hyderabad. There was a house in Mumbai with my father's name, but it was no longer home.

In the fourteen years that I spent in the United States, plus the five years after moving to Hyderabad, I had lost touch with many of the school and college friends I had grown up with.

Although a handful still lived in Mumbai, most had moved to other cities or countries. Perhaps they still remained in contact with each other via Facebook, but I was not on Facebook.

People claimed that Facebook had restored long lost connections and revived old relationships, but I had intentionally stayed away. Given my personal situation, I was not inclined to disclose personal details. Reluctant to admit my marital status or reveal the state of my finances (or lack thereof) or the true state of my mind, I preferred to keep a low profile, or rather, no profile.

My life kept me busy. I had neither the time nor patience to scroll through pictures of romantic dinners and expensive shopping trips or to chase a vicarious thrill by stalking others on exotic holidays. My to-do list was long and time was short.

If someone was looking for me, they would have to find me the old-fashioned way: in person.

I tried to keep my business trips within India short. When possible, I would fly in and out the same day, but if not, I booked a room at a hotel, keeping the entire visit strictly professional instead of piling on with friends or relatives.

It gave me a break from my own home routine but also from inquisitive questions about whether I was actually divorced or still separated and what was the difference between the two.

So, Mumbai, despite being my hometown, became just another business destination.

After finishing my guest lecture at Xavier's College, I took a taxi straight to the airport instead of lingering at old haunts where I had spent many happy evenings or exploring the profusion of new malls that had not existed in my childhood.

As I walked toward the departure gate, I heard someone call my name. Was I imagining it?

I turned around to find Anuradha, a dear friend from school, looking at me with a smile. We had not seen each other in fifteen years. We had corresponded through handwritten letters in the first few years after I left Mumbai, but with both of us moving out of our last known physical addresses, we had lost touch. What were the odds of us meeting again in real life? Only serendipity could explain this phenomenon. We caught up excitedly on all that had transpired in the intervening years. I missed my flight, but I reclaimed a friend.

Childhood is a time of openness and acceptance, of gullibility and trust, of fun and friendships. The bonds formed in the early years of life remain strong because on some level you realize that you and the other person are bundles of pure potential. You don't know how you will turn out. What will you become? How will you see and how will you be seen by the world? Despite the unknowns, there is a nonjudgmental acceptance of each other.

I learned that when I met Anuradha. Later, she would review the draft of my divorce agreement and accompany me to the lawyer's office. Much later, she would play a big role when I embarked on the second chapter of my life. But for now, we had rediscovered each other.

Anuradha worked in Delhi, but her parents had retired in Hyderabad so she visited the city often. She joined the circle of friends who had spontaneously come together around me in the last three years.

Radha's unconditional support had saved me from being homeless. My newest friends and neighbors, Kiran and Kumari, had helped me settle into the new neighborhood. Shailaja had welcomed me into her home for sleepovers. Anu had given me practical advice and support to create a work life that was perfect for me. And the list kept increasing every day.

They say it's not easy to make friends in adulthood, but for me the opposite had been true.

Except for Anuradha, all the women who formed my inner circle were people I had not known in my childhood. The tsunami of my personal life had opened doors to new possibilities, and the crumbling of my life as I knew it had also broken down pretenses and barriers. I was once again a child, learning the ways of the world and how to be in it. I was once again a bundle of potential. This clean slate helped me rewrite my life and rewire new connections.

My new friends were special because they were open to seeing me as a whole person. I was not just a scientist or Shreya's mother or someone's soon-to-be-ex-wife. They did not label me.

Strong and vulnerable, determined but diffident, different but human. They saw me as I was: a work in progress. And they generously resolved to watch over me while I went through my metamorphosis. Was I extremely lucky in finding such a group? Absolutely.

In the three years since leaving my husband's house, I had reclaimed parts of my authentic self. I had discovered the optimistic, trusting young woman that I had once been. She had remained dormant under layers of social conditioning but was still living and breathing deep inside.

I accepted the imperfections and broken parts of myself and in the process learned to accept the beauty in my brokenness.

Those who saw themselves reflected in the scattered pieces of my exposed life felt drawn, in spite of themselves, to play a part in my healing. Every friend I made in those years helped and healed me in myriad ways.

    I was not alone. I was not the only one who was struggling. We were all in it together. Unknowingly, we buoyed each other up, staying steadfast at times, becoming flexible when needed. They were my supporters and cheerleaders, my safety net and my safe nest. I did not have a husband, but I was blessed with many other nurturing relationships that enriched my life.

Taking the driver's seat

No man is an island ~ John Donne

One rainy Tuesday morning, Shreya and I woke up late—perhaps the alarm didn't ring or I may have hit snooze a few times. The reason didn't matter. What mattered was that we were late for school. Always anxious when things didn't go as planned, Shreya was extra worried because she had a test every Tuesday morning.

"Let's go, the school bus won't wait for us," Shreya said. It was fifteen minutes past the usual pick-up time. A call to the bus conductor confirmed my fears. We had missed the bus at our usual stop. How could I transport my child to school, which was several kilometers away?

"I can't miss the test," Shreya wailed. "I have to go to school!"

It would be impossible to get a car or taxi at this early hour in the pouring rain. There was a slim chance that we could intercept the bus on the main road once it meandered through the smaller streets in the neighborhood and worked its way to the highway, but we would be fully drenched by then!

From my doorstep, I could see my car, a pale blue Hyundai Accent, parked outside the garage like a forgotten elephant, sad and unused. It had been part of my compensation, a sort of a low-interest loan for a depreciating asset given by my employer. The monthly payments were deducted from my paycheck. The company had also paid a part of my driver Raju's salary.

On my last day at work, I had paid the remaining loan balance and transferred the car ownership to my name. Since I did not need a driver, I let Raju go, much to his relief. He had stayed out of a sense of loyalty but knew he could earn more with a different employer. He kindly offered to come by on Sundays, if needed, but I thanked him and wished him well. Since then, the car had been periodically cleaned but never used.

In the five years since my return to India, I had not taken the driver's seat once. I had truly enjoyed the perk of having a driver.

I looked longingly at my car through the curtain of rain. I couldn't drive. Not in the chaos of traffic in India. And certainly not in this weather.

Across his well-tended garden, I saw my neighbor looking out his window, watching us hesitate on our doorstep. We waved to him each morning as he prepared for his morning walk around our tree-lined neighborhood, and I had helped the elderly couple with internet banking and collected their mail in the months while they were away visiting their children in the United States. Should I ask him for a favor? I didn't have much time.

I took a deep breath and walked over, cowering under an umbrella.

"Hello Uncle. Shreya missed the school bus. Can you please drop us at the main intersection by the movie theatre? She may be able to catch the bus there."

He quickly pulled his Maruti Zen out of his garage and drove us to the designated pick-up point on the school bus route. We made it just in time. As Shreya waved to me with a relieved smile, I waved back with mixed feelings.

I had averted a minor crisis that day. But how much longer could I rely on the kindness of neighbors?

I would have to learn to drive again, this time in India.

Learning to drive had been one of my thrilling accomplishments in the United States. In my fourteen years there, I had driven over 100,000 miles. In India, cars were driven on the left side of the road but that did not worry me. The mechanics of driving were familiar to me. But driving in India required more than mere skill. It required nerves.

The Mumbai highway, an eight-lane road with no lane markings, buzzed with traffic that consisted of bicycles, motorcycles, cars, trucks, school buses, and a variety of stray animals right outside the quiet neighborhood where I lived. To get to any place in the city, I would have to learn to navigate the most congested part first.

Many years ago, a driving instructor had taught me how to merge into high-speed traffic on the freeways in the United States, but now I would have to strategize the best way to merge into the driving lanes in India.

One bright summer morning when traffic was light and school buses were off the roads, I sat in my car and practiced shifting gears with my left hand. I slowly pulled out on my street and held my breath as I inched toward the dreaded main road.

A few pedestrians, cattle, and stray dogs watched me intently as I began to drive Shreya to the swimming complex located about ten kilometers away. The road was deserted except for occasional trucks carrying cargo across state lines. I held the steering wheel tightly the entire time until we reached the spacious parking lot. As I pulled into a safe spot, a feeling of freedom coursed through me.

I watched Shreya swim the length of the Olympic-sized pool, her legs and arms lengthening in the water. As the simmering sun rose in the sky, I thought back to the days when I would drive little Shreya to Catherine's house and to the Santa Clara swimming pool.

As an infant, soaking in her little tub had calmed her down. By the time she was three years old, she was swimming confidently, propelling her tiny body through the water. Her first swimsuit had a blue and white checked pattern and a slice of watermelon on the front, a fruit that she loved. Even though the past was filled with unpleasant memories, there were fun moments to remember as well. Watching Shreya swim in the large rectangular pool brought back a wave of something akin to peace and gratitude.

By the time we left the pool, the sun was scorching and traffic on the roads had increased: buses plying workers to factories, private vehicles heading to offices, and young couples on motorbikes.

But there was room for my car too. I had a right to occupy the road as much as everyone else. Instead of being a helpless woman in the ocean of traffic, I saw myself as one with my car. My size and confidence instantly increased to the size of the four-door sedan that I was driving. With that subtle shift in mindset, I changed gears and merged across lanes, just as I had done over the years in the United States.

Driving skills, just as other survival skills, were ingrained in me, regardless of my awareness of their existence.

I had not learned to ride a bicycle with confidence, but I had learned to drive.

From the first two-door sporty Datsun in which I had learned to shift gears to a pale green Honda Accord sedan, a hatchback Toyota Camry, and a huge Isuzu Rodeo SUV, I had driven a variety of vehicles. A sabbatical from driving had not taken away my comfort with driving.

I didn't know then that driving in India would help me develop a steadfast mind like an archer, capable of staying calm and focused amid the mayhem of traffic.

Who could have predicted that soon I would gather enough confidence to drive to temples and train stations, shopping malls and offices? In the years to come, I would drive my father to the hospital after his heart attack, drive Shreya and her friends to school during unexpected transport strikes, and one day find the courage to step into a car showroom and buy my first car. Alone.

In the months after the German carmaker set up shop in Hyderabad, I passed the Volkswagen dealership located beside the green canopy of KBR Park in Jubilee Hills several times. The Vento, a model explicitly launched for the Indian market, was in the news. I read articles comparing it to the more popular Honda City, a vehicle favored among buyers looking for a car in the same price range.

One Christmas Eve, I entered the showroom for a closer look at available models. I had never before in my life studied, selected, and paid for a car myself.

Content to watch car-buying transactions, I had been happy to have access to a car, a prerequisite to move freely in the United States. I had never considered a car to be a personal statement or an object to be envied or coveted.

The Vento was the first car that I had researched. I knew the price I could afford, the color I liked, and the options that I needed to negotiate. But I wanted to test drive it first.

The salesman looked around to check if I was with someone. Upon my insistence he referred me to the manager, a suave, well-dressed young man.

"I want to test drive the Vento," I said

"Automatic, Madam?" he questioned.

"No, manual transmission," I replied.

"Who will drive, Madam?" he asked, his tone conveying his doubts about my abilities.

"I will," I replied firmly.

His incredulous expression would have been funny if it hadn't been so overtly sexist. He hesitated briefly before handing over the keys. I couldn't expect him to know that in my new life I was chef, chauffeur, working woman, mother, daughter, neighbor, friend. Driving was just one of those things I had mastered.

Moving toward meditation

Listen to the wind—it talks. Listen to the silence—it speaks. Listen to your heart—it knows ~ Native American Proverb

At Shobha's weekly study group, I met Meena, a young woman who was struggling with obesity and self-esteem issues. I admired her for exploring new ways of self-improvement that included physical, emotional, and spiritual avenues.

"I am learning meditation from the Brahmakumaris center," Meena mentioned one day. "I'm finding it very useful."

I had come across the Brahmakumaris, an organization that seemed to be comprised almost exclusively of women. They supported schools and led several initiatives in various communities.

I had been curious about these women in white sarees who spoke softly and moved serenely in the mad rush of urban life. They reminded me of the nuns at my school back in Mumbai who appeared as beacons of peace, even to my child self.

Was it because these women were free from the pressures of family life, with no husband or kids or other petty preoccupations? Or was it the unified energy of the group to which they belonged that granted them this gentle halo? I wondered if finding purpose that transcended the daily squabbles of quotidian life made them special.

I watched Sister Shivani, the spokesperson for the organization, who appeared in a short interview every evening on television and answered questions in an easy-to-understand way. She spoke about meditation and encouraged listeners to try the free seven-day course offered at their centers.

When Meena offered to accompany us for the initial session, it seemed like the right time to overcome my inhibitions. Instead of being thrust alone into deep dark woods teeming with dangerous thoughts, this time I would have support.

The early sessions of silent attention to my breath to still the butterfly mind showed me glimpses of all that I feared. I cried when I relived my mother's death. I choked at the return of hurtful words that had been exchanged during the years when my marriage slowly disintegrated. I felt a fresh stab of pain when I realized I could never get a chance to change those unhappy years.

Meditation made me sick.
Meditation made me mad.
Meditation made me sad.

A part of me knew that I needed this internal churning to push out my anger and release my resentment, to settle scores at the energy level, and to heal wounds rather than just seal them with time, as I had been doing until that point. So, I persisted.

After seven days of diligently attending sessions at the center, I practiced at home. I sat on my yoga mat each morning for longer periods of time. Some days I felt light but on other days I felt a little disoriented. I learned to feel comfortable in my own company. I spoke less, I listened more. I sensed others and I understood myself.

Meditation didn't work any miracles. Miracles happen in an instant of faith. The skeptic in me demanded proof.

One day, my printer started beeping. It was a paper jam. I opened the front and back panels and pried out pieces of paper but was unable to locate the exact cause. The printer kept beeping. I figured I had to take it to the service center, but the printer was heavy and the service center was far away. I hated the thought of having to lug this heavy equipment around the city. After multiple attempts during the day to identify the source of the problem, I gave up.

My last thought before falling asleep was about the beeping printer. I woke up with a single crystal-clear thought: "read the manual." Like Elizabeth Gilbert's scene in *Eat, Pray, Love* where she is lying on the bathroom floor in a helpless heap and hears, "go back to bed Liz," I felt like I was being given an anticlimactic resolution to an annoying problem.

I shook my head. Perhaps I had been dreaming. But the instruction felt insistent, as if someone had commanded those instructions into my ear. I found the manual and skipped to the troubleshooting section. I had missed one simple step while trying to identify the location of the paper jam and once I completed that step, the printer began working again.

Perhaps this had nothing to do with meditation, but the practical solution to a small but vexing problem showed me how my intuitive mind had come to my rescue when my logical mind had stalled.

Meditation gave me hope.

Meditation pointed toward a way.

Meditation showed me not just how to live my life but also how to think about life itself.

Perhaps the scientific method didn't apply to all situations. When logic failed, I could choose to sit, close my eyes, and wait for guidance. Often, the solution would present itself without great struggle. The trick was to still the conscious mind and allow myself to be led. The answer usually flowed in the lower subconscious depths. If I let the ripples settle, the answer rose to the top. Things would unfold exactly as they needed to. And with that knowledge, the tentacles of stress around my neck and shoulders eased.

It took more than motherhood to move me toward meditation. I first had to lose things—my mother, my marriage, my cynicism. I had to make life-changing decisions. Yet I moved, step by step, into the unknown inner world. Hesitatingly. Skeptically. Slowly.

Growing up

I may not have gone where I intended to go, but I think I have ended up where I needed to be ~ Douglas Adams

For the most part, I considered myself lucky. Even after giving up my job, my consulting business was doing reasonably well. Even though Amma was gone, I had Dada. I also had friends I could count on. But I still needed to face the consequences of my decision by myself.

On the day I received the first draft of the divorce application, my first feeling was relief. After years of being on the fence, I was finally on a path that was now irreversible. The moment felt important. Yet I felt alone. Within my family, I had claimed many firsts: first one to drive a car, first woman to earn a doctorate, and now I would be the first divorcee. Relief was replaced by regret.

There was no honor or pride in claiming this spot. It was a badge of failure. Like my height and skin color that were intrinsic to me, attributes that I could not change, this would become an identifying characteristic etched into my psyche forever. Is this what I really wanted?

I recalled an early conversation with Sunil the counselor: "Do you have any happy memories of your marriage?"

"Yes," I answered in a heartbeat.

"Tell me about them," he said.

I recounted the memorable visit to New York City on a freezing December afternoon just before my first Christmas in the United States. The city looked festive, lit up for the holiday season in the early darkness of a winter night. At the top of the World Trade Center building, which supposedly had the best view of the city, there was zero visibility.

We could only see our faces reflected in the thick glass. We stepped out of the building, disappointed. We drove over to Rockefeller center, which looked like a postcard for a winter wonderland, glittering with a towering Christmas tree that was surrounded by skaters. The bull of Wall Street looked forlorn and imposing. Steam gushed out of underground vents, startling me with their sudden shoosh.

When spring arrived, we returned to the city and visited the Statue of Liberty. Our friends from New Jersey visited us in DC for the cherry blossom festival. Years later, we soared in a hot air balloon over vineyards in Napa, took a helicopter ride over the Grand Canyon, and took pictures of Paris from the top of the Eiffel Tower.

The most unforgettable and miraculous memory, of course, was the sight of an aloof husband transforming to a doting father in a blink of an eye in the delivery room in California.

Of course, there were many.

Sunil observed me closely but didn't say much.

Changing my narrative from one of complaint and dissatisfaction to a more positive one changed my mood, but it didn't change all the other negatives that had tipped the balance of our marital life into dysfunction. Memories of good times were a reminder that life cannot be measured in purely black and white terms. The good and bad coexist in a tenuous equilibrium that is always in flux.

All of this didn't change the fact that I had to prepare for a meeting with the lawyer to discuss the terms of the divorce.

I knew it would be best to leave my family out of legal discussions. My brothers had busy lives. My recently widowed father was already grappling with a major life change that had taken away not just his wife but separated him from his beloved Mumbai. From being the patriarch of his family, he had become a temporary visitor in the homes of his caring yet distracted children.

It was time for me to run on my own. I needed a second opinion on the draft petition that had been sent to me.

I had remained in touch with Anuradha after our serendipitous meeting at the Mumbai airport. While we may have exchanged books and hung out at each other's home as schoolgirls, we had each borne our share of family responsibility in the decades since those happy days. I called her with a big ask.

"Would you mind taking a look at the draft of my divorce papers? And come with me to the lawyer's office?" I asked hesitantly, not sure if she would be willing to involve herself so deeply into this. I was prepared to do it alone if she refused.

"Of course," she replied, without a moment's hesitation.

Knowing that she had my back made me strong. I didn't speak much at the first awkward meeting with the lawyer.

All I wanted was Shreya's custody, which to my great surprise (and relief) had been assigned to me in the first draft. I agreed to not ask for anything else, not even a share of the house that had been built with our joint savings. There wasn't much to discuss except a quick exit.

"We will file the mutual consent petition in family court soon. Then it goes into a six-month waiting period," the lawyer said. Six more months!

We had been living apart for years, except for the brief, disastrous interlude. But the law was not adept at nuances. Although it could be expedited, the suggestion was to wait.

A few weeks later, Shailaja accompanied me to family court to formally file the papers. Eight months later, when the decree was granted, Radha stood with me as I signed the paper in the presence of the judge.

After nineteen years, six months, and eighteen days of being legally married, a sad looking piece of paper erased almost half of my life.

I had not worked this long and this hard at anything in my life. The years pursuing a PhD, the effort of tackling infertility, and the travails of being a working mother—none of it compared to this pain of abject failure.

Who could I blame? My father? The surviving parent who had supported the arranged marriage that had ended like this?

Who could I rage against? Fate? For handing me these lousy cards and setting me up for failure?

How would any of it help?

Growing up requires many things. Forgiveness is foremost—of self, of others. Forgiveness and acceptance of what is.

I was officially a divorcee. I had to accept it. I had to grow up.

"Is it done?" Dada asked when I stepped in through the door.

"Yes," I replied, our gazes meeting.

He looked at me for a long moment and nodded.

At that moment, I became an adult.

Marking anniversaries

~

*Should you shield the valleys from the windstorms,
you would never see the beauty of their canyons*
~ Elisabeth Kübler-Ross

Dates marked on a calendar are like babies: innocent and untainted. When we assign significance to one particular date—a wedding day for instance—we expand its notional value, even if it is precious only to us. The value of a day (or a baby) increases in proportion to our attachment to it.

What about divorce then? What remains when the event that gave a particular day special significance ceases to be a happy one? Are we supposed to rewind the film of our life to a point in the distant past, erase the intervening years from memory, and pretend it was just a nightmare that didn't really happen?

Like injuries that leave no scar, I had no visible reminder of the pain and trauma I had suffered in my marriage.

In the years we had been together, since my birthday fell four days after the wedding day, the anniversary had always eclipsed my birthday.

It had seemed excessive to buy lavish presents or to go out for dinner for two occasions so close together. Plus, Diwali usually fell within two weeks of these dates, making the larger public celebration one worth marking instead of our own private one.

On my twenty-second birthday, riding in a car decorated with flowers, I had looked across at my new husband with hope, expecting to step into a friendship that would last longer and be more intimate than any other relationship in my life.

He had been a catalyst for much of my transformation. By pushing me to explore Washington DC in the first week after my arrival on a cold winter day, he had enabled my curiosity. By insisting I learn to drive a car as soon as the first cherry blossoms peeked from the barren trees around the Jefferson memorial, he had given me the confidence to move around a vast country built for long drives.

Ironically, his detachment made me stronger. When I felt ill, I drove myself to the clinic. I took over responsibility for the home, for our child, for paying bills, and all the other work that goes into maintaining a home. When we went through our silent phases, I found a group of young mothers who supported me unconditionally. When I left his home, I didn't miss him much.

Yet, there were shared memories that would forever be etched into my memory. I would never forget the beads of sweat on his forehead, sparkling in the bright lights of the delivery room, his hands shaking with awe and fear at the prospect of having to cut the umbilical cord attached to our child who had just entered the world.

We exchanged a glance. He took the scissors from the nurse and responding to my encouraging nod, he severed the cord that tethered our newborn child to my body.

And finally—finally—that moment when he looked at the gooey dark-haired bundle with flailing arms and legs who was his and mine and fell wordlessly in love with her.

For all that we didn't have, we would always have her. The horizontal line that connected our two parallel lines and made the letter "H"—H for happy. Now we would be a happy family, or so I thought.

I was wrong. Our child was like a flower in the garden that we each tended to with affection and love, never sparing a thought to the other person who contributed to her well-being. Even under the same roof, we hardly communicated with each other except for the practical aspects of our life as working parents. On good days, we stayed silent. On bad days, we fought.

On the sixteenth anniversary of our wedding, I had walked out of a house that I once hoped would be our forever home.

My subsequent birthdays had carried a nasty aftertaste—a salty, sour combination of curdled hope and innocence.

Exactly three years later, we formally filed for divorce in family court.

Now that would forever be a day I would not forget.

What should I call this day? Wedding Day? Divorce Day?

No matter its name, from then on it would always be a bittersweet day. The final step would take six more months, but it would give legal sanction to my situation.

It was a day filled with relief and grief in equal measure.

I mourned for the fact that we would not create memories together.

I rejoiced for the fact that we would not create more memories together.

I cried because both of those opposing states were true.

Elisabeth Kübler-Ross describes the five stages of grief (denial, anger, bargaining, depression, and acceptance) that are usually associated with the death of a loved one.

But what about the end of a relationship? Was there a process or ritual that would help me navigate the choppy waters of a major life event that no one wanted to talk about?

When Amma died, my brothers had been instructed to perform a series of rituals that lasted several days to help her soul make its final journey. It had been arduous, the process of letting go of someone who had given you life and given her life over to you. In the days following her cremation, I had grieved: sobbing loudly and silently, touching her sarees and her kitchenware, reading her neat handwriting, and studying the last unfinished Sudoku grid that she had attempted.

The religious rituals and Sanskrit mantras had helped, even though I could not comprehend them because the rituals allowed me to devote myself to the only task at hand, the task of grieving. The undeniable public fact of death allowed people around me to give me the space I needed. Plus, my siblings suffered equally.

In the first year after Amma's death, Dada and I had one thing in common: we had both lost a spouse. My father, although stoic on the outside, chose to grieve in his own silent way. I envied him because he could openly express his grief if he chose to do so. I could not.

With my divorce, I had to keep both my grief and relief private. No one, not even my closest family members, could comprehend the complicated feelings that washed over me. No one I knew had experienced this kind of loss.

There was no social ritual to indicate that I had undergone a major life event. No forty days of rest as after childbirth, no forty days of mourning after death. There was no symbolic act of closure.

Like the divorce, the absence of closure would be a unique cross for me to bear.

Embracing my single life

*Compatibility is an achievement of love;
it shouldn't be its precondition ~ Alain de Botton.*

"The chikungunya virus is spread by the bite of an infected mosquito," says the CDC website. While it does a good job of listing symptoms, diagnosis, and treatment, it does not describe the havoc it creates in daily life.

I could not remember when the mosquito bit us, but like dominos—first Dada, then Shreya, and finally I—we all collapsed in a puddle of pain. The fever was manageable, but the joint pain brought me to my knees.

Shreya recovered quickly, eager to return to school. She had exams and didn't want to miss them. While she got ready for school, I usually prepared her lunch, combed her hair into two braids, and accompanied her to the bus stop, a task that was delegated to Dada whenever he visited us. But not today. He was having trouble recovering from the nasty virus.

My fever had subsided, but the secondary effects persisted. Joints and bones that I didn't know existed screamed in pain, most loudly during the first hour after waking.

Sleep made them extra stiff. It felt as though they were cast in some kind of a frozen mold that required gentle thawing in the morning.

I stood up gingerly, bracing for the razor-like shards of pain to rise up from my feet to my head. My fingers looked normal but felt like gnarled tree trunks, bent out of shape by nature. I could neither lift nor push anything heavy. Even rotating the lid of the Nutella jar seemed too big a task for my puny fingers. How could I get Shreya ready for school?

"Why don't you make a ponytail today?" I suggested. She happily obliged. I shuffled to the kitchen to look for an easy substitute for her favorite snack. She chose to eat cereal with milk, and I put some grapes and a small pack of Oreos in a box. Shreya walked with an extra spring in her step as I accompanied her to the bus stop, delighted by the ponytail that bobbed up and down on her head.

"Can I make a ponytail every day?" she asked. I smiled at the ease with which she had embraced this change along with everything else in the past few years. But inside, I was seething.

I decided to walk around the neighborhood before returning home.

The morning's episode had brought home the full import of what my life ahead would look like. I would be single. A single parent. But most of all, I would be alone.

I had no one to call if I needed a ride from the airport. I did not have a shoulder to cry on when bad news arrived. I would not have someone to celebrate happy moments with. I could not count on someone to carry the load when I was sick, like now.

Wedding vows, in any culture or language, speak of being together in sickness and in health.

There is an assumption that you will receive love and thrive in the constant presence and support of the person with whom you are joined together in matrimony, no matter the weather or circumstance. By committing to spending your life together, you are promising one thing: to be around.

Yet there is no test to evaluate how you fare over the years. No annual appraisal. No audit. No oversight. No corrective action. Every couple settles into their own normal.

Some are like twins, glued together, echoing each other. Others are like siblings, squabbling and jostling but united in the most important tasks. Yet others are rarely seen together, like the sun and the moon in the sky, separate but linked nevertheless.

We had been like bad roommates, right from the early years. Living under the same roof, having practical but limited conversations about food or bills, trying hard to not step into the other's space.

At times, we had loud arguments, expressing our dissatisfaction and expectations of the other—hygiene factors, as management experts say. But at no point did we assume that we had any power over the other. There were no words of love or even tenderness.

Had he truly celebrated my achievements or showed up on days that held special significance for me? I had been alone at events where my accomplishments were being complimented and at family gatherings, like my brothers' weddings, where we were expected to show up as a couple. In every instance, I would dread the inevitable question of "where is your husband?"

Ask him yourself, I would respond curtly.

During the height of our infertility phase, I clearly recalled how I drove myself back from the clinic after an extremely painful hysterosalpingogram, as shockwaves of cramps coursed through my lower body.

How many times had I requested friends for a ride from the airport, or to pick up Shreya from day care if I was running late? I was still married then.

His callous behavior in the months after Amma's death showed me what I had been searching for all along—kindness.

I had expected kindness from my spouse.

Money I could make. Had I not left my lucrative career in the United States, given up every dollar I had earned during our marriage, and left the big, comfortable house in a posh area of Hyderabad to make a simple home in a distant suburb?

Physical help, the kind a man is typically expected to provide in a marriage, I had learned to outsource.

Emotional support had not been his strong suit in any case. I tended to have outbursts. He withdrew. I vented my feelings onto a page or to parents when feeling particularly low. He was averse to not just confrontation but also to communication.

"How was the chemistry between the two of you at the beginning of your relationship?"

Linda the facilitator had asked at the workshop in Palo Alto years ago.

Not only had we lacked chemistry, we lacked compatibility. We had not been able to find a wavelength that matched both our needs.

None of my angry thoughts were new. I had been mulling over the reason for the break in our marriage for years. A break implies there was a connection to begin with, but I understood now that there had never been a connection—not at the beginning when we were young strangers tied together by the bonds of marriage and not even after we became parents to a child who we both loved in our own imperfect ways.

I had accepted the lackluster state of our marriage as an unchangeable fact, like the laws of nature. But the mountain of resentment kept building each time I drove myself to the doctor, each time I called someone else for backup, each time I answered people who inquired about his absence.

I had been married, but I had also been alone the entire time.

There was nothing to mourn about my situation as a divorced woman because there was nothing more to lose.

All had been lost within the walls of the various houses that we had occupied over the years. Like two lost planets from different galaxies, we had orbited within a constrained space, straining against the pull of love for our child. But most of all, we had spent our energy trying to avoid collisions. Was that a life worth living?

I could live without chemistry but not without kindness.

Would he have helped me open the Nutella bottle this morning if we had been together? Maybe. Maybe not. It would have depended on the prevailing mood. On rare occasions, I would get support. Most often, I would be ignored. And, sometimes, I would be told to figure it out myself, particularly if the action was for my benefit.

I returned home with one clear thought: we were both right, but we were not right for each other.

I was glad that I had put myself out of this misery called marriage.

V

SOARING

Owning my name

It ain't what they call you, it's what you answer to
~ W. C. Fields

I have two names—two first names, two last names.

Most people call me Ranjani.

When Amma was a teenager, she heard a devotional song in praise of Goddess Parvati that was set to the soulful melody that is called Ranjani raga in Carnatic music. Amma was captivated. She decided then that she would name her daughter Ranjani.

I also have another name, the name by which I was known in school and college. This name originally belonged to my father's sister, the one who died young. When I was born, my paternal grandmother suggested naming me for her deceased daughter. Amma resisted. Fearful of attracting misfortune and untimely death to her newborn and determined to act upon her long-held wish about naming her daughter, Amma refused to budge.

Torn between the wishes of wife and mother, Dada did what he thought was reasonable.

He entered both names in the school register. By making both names official, he saddled his only daughter with the burden of two names. As I grew up, I had a nebulous awareness of the two parts that comprised me, two sides that were complementary, not congruent.

When I got married, I needed a passport to leave for the United States. I could choose to rearrange my first names and take the same last name as my new husband, but I was undecided. Dada stepped in once more. Using the newly issued marriage certificate, he officially changed my name again. My shiny passport had my picture but seemed to belong to a stranger. The two first names switched places but stayed and I had a new last name.

My new name marked my entry into a foreign country. Here I was a wife. I was once again a student, but now my graduate school classmates called me Ranjani. With time, I grew into my name and life grew like a tightly wrapped shell around this central kernel of my identity. I published scientific papers, acquired a green card, and later wrote freelance articles for local magazines. As far as my name went, my personal and professional identities finally merged. I was no longer the split twin.

Years later, when Shreya was born, I checked the spellings on the form for her birth certificate. It felt good to see that our new family of three was united in one way; we all bore the same last name.

The story of my marriage and motherhood is not unusual: a life defined by a name, a name conferred by someone other than me. Most women I knew had taken on their husband's name either at the time of the wedding or after the birth of their children. A few had retained their maiden name, with a handful agonizing over the decision.

I had lived within the confines of familiar social mores, not overthinking the consequences of my choice of name in a future I could not foresee. I didn't get to pick any of my names, but I could decide what I, the person who bore the name, did with them.

The dictionary defines the noun form of the word "divorce" as "legal dissolution of a marriage by the court or other competent body." However, as a verb, it means "to separate or dissociate (something) from something else, typically with an undesirable effect."

When I received the divorce decree, I found myself at yet another crossroads. Changing my name would help me cement the divorce by allowing me to dissociate from the constant reminder of the long but unpleasant phase of my life. Yet I continued to use the name that was on my first passport, the name that I had identified with in adulthood as my formal name. I kept the name because it was easier to do so.

I had the legal right to hold on to my married last name, irrespective of my marital status. As a career woman, it maintained the continuity of my professional credentials. But more importantly, as Shreya's primary parent, it marked the two of us as a cohesive unit.

Like GPS coordinates, my two last names pointed to my location on the planet for an equal number of years.

A name after all is a label as personal as "sweetheart" that a lover may use or as distant as a "hey you" that a stranger in a crowd may call out. But a name is more than a label. It is an inheritance that is uniquely your own. It is the primary way in which you respond to the world and the lens through which the world sees you. It defines you, shapes you, and grounds you. It is the one right you take for granted from the time you start interacting with society.

Decades ago, Pulitzer Prize–winning author Anna Quindlen wrote about holding on to her maiden name after marriage "…. *it so happens that when it came to changing my name, there was no consideration, rational or otherwise. It was mine. It belonged to me. I don't even share a checking account with my husband. Damned if I was going to be hidden beneath the umbrella of his identity.*"

Although she felt left out when she had children who bore the same last name as her husband, she declared, "*I made my choice. I haven't changed my mind. I've just changed my life.*"

I came across a blogger who wrote about deciding to take on her husband's name after having two children. "*It will draw me, on paper, into the fold of our little foursome. We will be our unit. I don't know why it matters to me that the world sees that. But for some reason, it does. I want the world to know we're a little family of four. That means playing by the world's rules. That means all having the same name.*"

The sense of agency inherent in the opinions of the two women is empowering. But I am at the opposite end of the spectrum from them. They are contemplating their name change as a consequence of their union while I am pondering over the next steps following the dissolution of my marriage. If I change my name, what else will change?

The city I grew up in changed names a few years ago, discarding the Anglicized "Bombay" in favor of the original name, "Mumbai." What changed? Not much.

Shouldn't the new name have symbolized some change? An improved version, a makeover, a different avatar perhaps?

The city itself went on unconcerned. Its population density, chaos, and overall entropy kept increasing as always. The Bombay of my childhood and the Mumbai of today are different, but it has nothing to do with the change of its name.

Change happens as it inevitably does.

The city evolved in response to external factors. It had grown, decayed, resurrected, and renewed itself in many ways, undocumented by name boards, unsung by media. Mumbai remained the whirring, buzzing megapolis I loved, filled with its effervescent energy, a testament to its irrepressible DNA that adapts and survives, unfazed by natural disasters and man-made terrors.

Unlike cities, a person's name change generally signifies a life change. In my case, my life changed while my name stayed the same.

I had once been a naive young woman who left behind her maiden name and her father's home. I had been the disgruntled wife who struggled for years in an unhappy marriage. I had been the grieving daughter who mourned the death of her mother. But I was also the resilient woman who decided to walk out into uncharted territory as a single parent. At various points, my life changed but my DNA remained indomitable. My unchanged core had adapted to every situation and environment. Did the label really matter?

Occasionally, I considered dropping the last name entirely, like Madonna, but I was no celebrity.

A name change is more than just a superficial statement. It is serious business. And I had no energy to pursue the associated administrative paperwork that was needed. There was so much else to figure out. Plus, I lacked the conviction to follow through.

I am more than the combination of words by which I am addressed. My personal identity is more than just my name. Like Bombay, my evolution will continue, unseen and unannounced. The name by which I am known is mine, and any decision that I need to make is a personal one. One day, I might tackle the conundrum, but until then, I would stick with it and own it.

Happy Days

How we live our days is how we live our lives
~ Annie Dillard

I understood the meaning of these words long before I came across this quote.

At Shoppers Stop, Shreya and I picked out letters that spelled our names from a pile of colorful glossy alphabet tiles. We were getting ready to move into a new home: our home. One that I owned, that had my name, not just on the formal papers and the bank loan documents but also on the name board in the lobby of the brand new ten-floor apartment building. A three-bedroom corner apartment on the fifth floor belonged to me. The space and the debt were mine. No one could ask me to leave this house. I would never be homeless again.

The check I had written to the builder five years earlier, days before moving out of the house that I had shared with my husband, had not been wasted. It had taken time, but things had finally swung in my favor. In a weird twist of fate, the worldwide fallout following the 2008 recession turned out to be a boon for me.

After three years of no progress, the builder had finally resolved the land litigation case and moved this construction project to the top of his priority list. In the same time frame, I had gone from having practically nothing in my bank account to a decent nest egg. The consulting work was not as predictable as a regular paycheck, but money kept coming in. Home loans were available at phenomenally low interest rates. I was in a good place to pay the builder as per the payment schedule. I borrowed a small sum from the bank that I could easily repay with my current level of earnings.

Dada had suffered a heart attack two months earlier but had recovered quickly after the angioplasty. He sat beside the driver of the moving truck that transported my belongings from the big rented house to my new cozy apartment.

On the day of the housewarming, my home filled with the cadence of Vishnu Sahasranamam and the good wishes of the precious group of people who had enabled my journey to independence. My brothers, two aunts, and a cousin came with their families. But the larger group in attendance were the circle of friends I had made and relied upon during the difficult years.

A few days before the gathering, Shailaja and I had made a special trip to Pochampalli, a town famous for its uniquely crafted sarees, located about one hundred kilometers away.

"You don't have to give such expensive gifts to everyone who comes," Dada said.

"I want to give my friends something nice to mark this happy occasion. They were there for me when the days were tough. Today is a happy one. I want them to remember this day when they wear the saree," I smiled and replied.

Dada looked at me with surprise and pride.

"You are a much better person than me, for thinking such thoughts. I know it has not been easy for you. But you have done the right thing because I can finally see the smile on your face. In all the years of your marriage, I had forgotten your smile," he said, teary-eyed.

Coming from Dada, the words were highly unusual. My parents belonged to a generation that didn't believe in openly praising children lest they become arrogant. But hearing this from him brought tears to my eyes. I hugged him, knowing how hard it must have been for a father to watch his daughter suffer.

The memorable days are few. Most days are a blur of chores and errands and activities that don't really add up to anything significant. But there is value in savoring the simple joys that each day brings. There is power in being able to choose not just your home and its contents but how you see your life and its context.

I had chosen a bright green paint for the far wall in the master bedroom, carefully placed minimal furniture in the living room, and had a smooth granite countertop installed in my kitchen. Every room had a bookshelf—my favorite piece of furniture. In my assigned parking spot in the basement, I proudly parked my new Volkswagen Vento. Radha helped me pick curtains and get them custom tailored. Shailaja and I chose cushion covers and bed sheets.

As the days went by, friends stopped over for impromptu lunches, and Shreya's classmates came for sleepovers. Sometimes Shreya and I played loud Bollywood music and danced. My home resounded with laughter and occasional arguments as Shreya and Dada fought over the remote for the new wall-mounted flat screen television that had been a housewarming gift from Dada.

Every time I walked into my home, I felt pride but also peace. Although I still lived in the same city as my ex-husband, I had come a long way since that scary day exactly five years ago when I had walked away from the security of an unhappy marriage and into a world of no guarantees.

I was the first person in my extended family to do so. With no step-by-step guidance or role models, I had stumbled and fallen and picked myself up. I had survived. I had thrived. All along, I had moved one day at a time, one considered step followed by another, one morning followed by another night. Each day had been an improvement from the day before.

I had lost my mother, resigned from my job, and dissolved my marriage the year I turned forty. Most importantly, I had given up on the myth of the happily ever after that is supposed to follow your wedding. Instead, I embraced the simple joy of the here and now.

From measuring my life in terms of milestones, I now tried to measure it in moments—those small pockets of time that float with great radiance even though they are embedded in the minutiae of life.

Singing along with Shreya as I drove her around town, making an unplanned stop at Baskin-Robbins, going away with friends for an impulsive girls-only holiday, indulging Shreya's fascination with earrings, attending a late evening concert at the Qutub Shahi tombs, heading to Charminar for night shopping during the month of Ramzan—there was so much joy to savor.

I had spent too many years of my adult life waiting for things to change, for him to change, for me to change. I had given over the energy of the present moment to the promise of a future that never arrived.

Not anymore.

I wanted to grab this moment, which was light and precious and fleeting. I could have done it all along, but it had taken me this entire journey to figure that out. Like Santiago in *The Alchemist* by Paulo Coelho, I had to make the journey in order to return home. Confident. Content.

Incorporating rituals

Our reality is not the infinitely stretching cosmos but the small part we choose to focus on ~ Haemin Sunim

Landing at the Washington Dulles International Airport on a Friday evening in December 1989 marked my first time being outside of my country. I picked up my luggage and scanned the crowded arrivals hall with a mixture of exhaustion, excitement, and dread. Except for my husband, who I had met twice before the ceremony, I did not know anyone in this new country. I was optimistically and naively embarking on my very own Bollywood-tinted version of "happily ever after," but it would be decades before I would understand that happiness does not come from a person or place.

When I opened the door to our apartment for the first time, I couldn't help but feel like I had just walked into a refrigerator, despite the dull brown carpet that lined every inch of the floor. An L-shaped sofa with grey plaid upholstery sat in a corner of the living room, a round glass-topped coffee table placed at one end.

The dining area was strewn with a few empty moving boxes. A new mattress lay on the floor in the bedroom. Why did this apartment seem more spacious than the one-bedroom flat in Mumbai that I had left behind?

The space that I had shared with two brothers, parents, and a grandmother had been cramped, but it had also been full of cozy conversations and accumulated memories that had enveloped me in a tight embrace.

Despite central heating, I was cold. I wrapped my shawl a little bit tighter around myself and peeped through the curtains into the silent winter night. Bare limbs extended from tall trees like hands reaching up for a warm hug.

"Does it snow here?" I asked, echoing the ignorance of people from tropical countries who romanticize snow, unaware of how ill-equipped they are to handle it.

"Sometimes," he replied.

When he left for work on Monday, I pulled back the curtains. Cars whizzed by at high speeds on a stretch of highway in the distance. The street outside was deserted. I looked up at the blue sky. A clear day did not mean a warm day, something I had learned over the weekend while walking around the Smithsonian trying not to shiver in the few minutes it took to get from one enclosed museum to another.

I missed the familiar sounds of vehicles honking, street vendors calling out their wares, and the noisy whistles of our pressure cooker back home. Silence was the only palpable presence within and outside the cold walls of our apartment.

Phone calls were expensive. In any case, the time difference was impractical for a call. I thought longingly of home, the bustle of my mother's kitchen with ribbons of sunlight streaming in through the large window.

Spicy aromas from Amma's stove would mingle with the long trails of jasmine-scented smoke billowing from incense sticks that Dada would light as part of his morning prayer routine. He would light lamps, chant prayers, and offer flowers to various deities arranged on the low altar.

It would be impossible to recreate the welcoming ambience of my mother's home in my windowless kitchen. Perhaps I could begin by setting up a space for prayer.

In Mumbai, our kitchen doubled as dining space during mealtimes and one corner was permanently dedicated to the altar. In the United States, space was not a constraint, but my kitchen with its smooth countertop was cluttered with unfamiliar appliances and lacked natural light.

By repurposing a sturdy moving box, I created a makeshift altar to hold my Ganesha idol and framed photographs of other gods and goddesses that had been packed into my suitcase along with a few kitchen utensils and a starter pack of spices. I chose an east-facing spot near the French doors leading out from the dining area to the balcony.

I laid out a red stole with a gold border on the box and layered it with sheets from the weekend's *Washington Post* to soak up spilt oil drops and collect hot embers of incense ash that would undoubtedly fall on it each day.

In my bulging suitcase I found a pair of silver lamps, a gift from my mother, who had thoughtfully included a pack of cotton wicks. I wondered if it was a silent request to initiate a time-honored tradition in my new home.

"Use sesame oil," she had advised. I knew the rest.

Each morning, Amma's day began with a series of unchanging rituals. She would wash the silver lamps with hot water to remove soot and oily residue. She would then scrub the brass lamps with tamarind and salt to reverse the inevitable oxidation and make them shine.

My grandmother would spend her afternoons making wicks from long skeins of unbleached cotton. Her deft fingers would shape them into little flowers, with sharp stalks and dandelion-like gossamer heads. She stored them in a biscuit tin to protect them from Mumbai's overpowering humidity.

Amma would pour a tablespoon of oil into the shallow cup of two lamps and slide the pointed end of each wick, letting it soak for a few moments. Through capillary action, the oil would permeate all the way to the head of the wick, which she would flatten into the cup. She would then strike a match and light the soggy shaft of each wick, which would quickly light up into a tiny oval flame that would burn steadily for at least an hour.

On school days, the two orbs of light and the sweet smell of incense would remind my brothers and me to quickly prostrate in front of the altar before racing out. In contrast, the evening ritual of lighting the lamps at dusk was more soothing.

In that ambiguous hour between day and night, I would sit beside Amma and recite prayers or listen to her sing *bhajans*. As the flames flickered and projected shadows on the walls, a nebulous peace would permeate our home with the lamp at the center of that aura.

At twenty-two, my move away from home had been a large leap into the unknown. I didn't know much. The country was as much of a mystery to me as the man I had married.

He watched me fill the silver lamps with cooking oil and immerse the cotton wick. We hadn't discussed religious rituals—though in truth we hadn't really discussed much of anything.

I asked him for matches, a common item in Indian kitchens. He hesitated, fearful of apartment rules, possible fire safety violations, and wall to wall carpeting. After a brief search, he found a lighter left behind by a previous roommate. It took a few attempts before I got it to work. I lit the lamp, said my prayers, and prostrated to Ganesha, requesting blessings for this new chapter of my life.

Fire is an important component of Hindu traditions. From the sacred fire around which you walk during your wedding to the final lighting of the funeral pyre, it occupies center stage at significant life events. On ordinary days you light an oil lamp as part of your daily practice.

The altar setup was my first step in setting up my own home, my first independent decision as a married woman.

In my sparkling new apartment in Hyderabad, a compact custom altar sat in a corner of the dining area, a gift from Shailaja, who had been my companion through a large part of my new life.

As I inaugurated the new altar by placing an idol of Ganesha and a pair of shiny silver lamps with cotton wicks, I thought back to the makeshift altar in that first apartment in Maryland and in all the other houses I had inhabited.

My "fairy-tale life" had included easy days as a carefree couple, mundane days in the lab as I pursued a PhD, agonizing days after a miscarriage, desperate days handling infertility, and one miraculous day when Shreya, our perfect baby girl was born.

As a family, we had survived disagreements, displacement, and disappointment, but we had failed to grow together as a couple. When I walked out that fateful day, I thought it was the final straw, but little did I know there was more to lose.

I lost my mother, the pillar of my confidence. I didn't know how to recreate my life. All I could do was what I had done each morning for all these years. Light my lamp. Every. Single. Day.

My life changed. My marital status changed. I changed. But my daily ritual stayed constant.

In the dull golden glow of the lamp at dusk, I chanted shlokas I had learned as a child. Or sat still while my mind buzzed with wordless questions. Sometimes I sent out wordless anguished requests, demanding explanations, seeking solutions. At other times, in the absence of a clear way forward, I firmly declared my willingness to understand the turmoil outside and inside me. In the presence of that gentle, flickering flame, I surrendered.

Lighting the lamp is an art. A ritual. A discipline.

For my mother, it was a religious practice. For me, it had begun as a way of holding on to what I knew when I didn't know anything else.

As with any ritual, the longer you do it, the more power it garners—from the act, from the faith, from the feeling.

Lighting the lamp became my anchor, and my focus, a deliberate act, and a resolution.

My mother taught me how to light the lamp. Life gave me a reason to do so. And in the process, it made me whole.

Grand gesture

Success is not final, failure is not fatal: it is the courage to continue that counts ~ Winston Churchill

My new Volkswagen Vento was my pride and joy. I smiled each time I saw it parked in its assigned spot in the basement of my new apartment. I decided to sell my old car that I had bought from my employer. It sold quickly for a decent sum.

"What are you planning to do with the money from the car sale?" Shailaja asked one day when we met for lunch.

"Haven't thought about it," I said.

"If you put it in the bank, it will merge with your savings, like a river flowing into the ocean, and disappear. Why don't you convert it into something else?"

"Like what?" I asked, curious.

"How about diamonds? Diamonds are forever, more reliable than husbands," she said with her trademark smile.

"You know I'm not big on jewelry," I replied.

"Don't think of it as jewelry. Think of it as an investment. Diamonds are a girl's best friend," she said.

I wasn't convinced. Yet, her words gave me pause. I wondered about jewelry and relationships and the connection between the two. I owned a ring with three sparkling diamonds that belonged to my maternal grandmother. It had fit me perfectly since I was a teenager, and after my grandmother's death, Amma gave it to me. After Amma's death, I inherited the pair of diamond earrings that she used to wear every day.

From the day I left my husband's house five years ago, I had stopped wearing the long gold *mangalsutra* that was the mark of a married woman.

At the time of the wedding, at the auspicious moment, my (ex) husband had tied two strands of string anointed with turmeric, each strung with a handful of gold and black beads with a pendant at the center, around my neck. In the weeks following the wedding, the string was substituted by sturdy gold chains.

One had alternating black and gold beads while the other was a thick gold rope. Each had one pendant, and I had alternately worn one or the other in the sixteen years we lived together.

I had no need for it now. Not the gold chains nor the pendants. They sat in a locker in the bank, a reminder and a warning.

"When you got married, I bought one new pendant for you. The second was the pendant that was on my mother's mangalsutra. I should not have done that," my mother had confessed a few months before her death.

My maternal grandmother's marital life had been full of strife. Married off at the age of nine, as was the custom then, she had gone from being the elder daughter of a wealthy family to the wife of a learned but impoverished man.

"My mother's unhappy marriage has cast a shadow on your marriage," Amma said, with an uncharacteristic catch in her voice. Amma was not superstitious, just sad at the way my life had turned out. No one, least of all your mother, wishes unhappiness for you. But Amma felt complicit in this aspect of my life.

What would Amma say if I decided to end the curse by destroying its symbol?

∞

Shailaja accompanied me to the row of jewelry shops in Punjagutta. Tanishq, Joy Alukkas, Kalyan—all the big-name stores sat next to each other with their glittering store fronts.

Uniformed guards stationed outside each store carefully watched the flow of customers. We entered Tribhuvandas Bhimji Zaveri, a Mumbai-based store where my parents had bought some of my wedding jewelry almost twenty years ago. The store had expanded its franchise and recently opened a branch in Hyderabad.

Although not fully convinced about buying jewelry for ostentation, I had learned that diversification of your portfolio was a sound practice. I owned a flat, a car, and had cash savings. I could justify the purchase of an expensive piece of jewelry as an investment. I entered the air-conditioned store with a practical thought.

"What would you like to buy?" Shailaja asked.

"Solitaire earrings?" I said, half questioningly to myself. I could wear those more often—smart, sparkly, and simple. Amma's traditional earrings with six diamonds each were better suited for special occasions.

"You already have earrings. Let's look at necklaces," Shailaja suggested.

I wasn't the diamond necklace-wearing type. Yet over the years, I had seen women who carried them well. Although not appropriate for daily use, it could be an expensive but elegant accessory, a statement piece that could draw attention without speaking a single word.

The salesperson was helpful. She brought out several options—some blingy, some sober, and some way over my budget. Finally, I laid my eyes on the perfect one: a strand of the right length with diamonds of the right size and sparkle, set in a simple, pleasing pattern.

I tried it on. It felt right. I moved my head to the right and the left in the small mirror. The diamonds sparkled in the flattering store lighting.

"How much?" I asked.

Of course, it was more expensive than my budget, which was equal to the money I had made from the sale of my car. I didn't want to dilute my savings to fund this purchase. The point was to convert one asset class (cash) into another (diamonds) to diversify my portfolio, not impoverish it by engaging in a vanity-driven exercise.

"What about your mangalsutra?" Shailaja asked me in a low voice. "Do you want to trade it in?"

In previous conversations, I had confided to Shailaja that the sight of my mangalsutra always made me sad.

"Let me think about it," I said to her. We left the store without a decision.

I went to the locker the next day and took a look at the mangalsutra pendants. As always, it brought back pangs of unhappiness and anxiety. I brought them home with me. There was much to unpack.

We returned the next day with the two pendants and the black and white beaded necklace to offer as a trade-in.

Along with the cash from the car sale, it added up to the exact amount required for the new diamond necklace. The deal was done.

There is change, and there is transformation.

Change is gradual, like the seasons and our bodies, like the inside-out change that my life had undergone in the last five years. It had been a slow, systematic process in which I added dimensions to myself by erasing old beliefs.

Transformation, on the other hand, is what happens to water when heated. At the boiling point, there is a dramatic conversion of the physical state. Although the atomic composition remains constant, the outer presentation changes radically. From being contained in a vessel, it expands to occupy all available space.

After leaving my marital home, I continued to be Ranjani at the molecular level, but I was a different person. It's tempting to use the analogy of a snake shedding its skin or the metamorphosis of a caterpillar to a butterfly, but the more suitable comparison is to an octopus that has lost its limb. A new limb grows back, but it requires great inner strength, time, and focus to rebuild after such a loss. It is tough but it is possible.

My past and its associated trauma would always remain a part of me, but it would not be the only thing to define me.

Like a child building a brand new toy with a heap of Lego blocks, I reassembled the useful pieces from the debris of my old life with patience, persistence, and a strong belief that a better life was possible. In doing so, I was able to reveal a new avatar of myself.

By turning in the last physical remnant of a relationship that was now legally severed, I made a grand gesture to the world and to myself that I had moved on.

Sometimes a physical act is necessary to declare with finality that you have reached a turning point. The public declaration is not just an announcement but an acceptance of the mantle that you have chosen, perhaps reluctantly and with great thought, but always with an awareness of what it entails.

There were many rites and rituals to mark birth and death and coming of age milestones, but for divorce there was nothing—neither in the religious nor spiritual realm—to mark completion of this phase of life. By turning in my mangalsutra and transforming it into an unrecognizable but undeniable asset externally, I was declaring that I was doing the same internally as well. It marked an end and a beginning.

The diamonds glittered and nodded in the bright store lighting. I made a promise to myself: whether or not I wore this necklace, I would always shine.

Later—much later—I would wear this necklace at an event where the brilliance of my smile would rival the sparkle of the diamonds. But that, as they say, is another story.

Also by Dr. Ranjani Rao

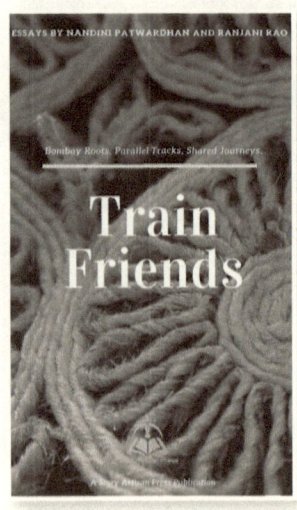

About the author

Dr. Ranjani Rao is a trained scientist, a self-taught writer, yoga practitioner, and lifelong learner committed to an apprenticeship in observation.

Ranjani is the author of three books. She is a regular columnist for The Straits Times, Singapore. Her award-winning commentaries and op-eds reflect her lived experiences in three countries and have appeared in several print and digital magazines and anthologies.

Originally from Mumbai, India, Ranjani spent several years in the USA and now lives in Singapore with her family. When not working or tackling the unread pile of books by her bedside, she goes for long walks in the nature reserve behind her home. She returns with either new ideas or pictures of wildlife that she shares on social media, much to the embarrassment of her children.

Acknowledgements

A book, like a baby, needs a village to achieve its full potential.

While this story was told from my point of view, it is only one way of illuminating a mosaic of memories created with the people whose life intersected with mine during a time of great turmoil. Big thanks to everyone named in these pages and those who supported me behind the scenes. Each step was possible because of you.

I owe a huge debt of gratitude to my parents for their unstinting support and to my brothers for their unwavering confidence in me. Everything else I owe to my daughter who has been my North Star since the day she was born. Her presence and support gave me the clarity and strength to keep moving.

This book was written after a decade of doubts and delays but then it came together magically in a few months.

A big thank you to Nandini Patwardhan for convincing me to write this book. Her ongoing friendship and wise counsel as a fellow writer and co-founder of Story Artisan Press has enriched my writing and publishing journey.

Thanks to my newsletter subscribers and beta readers for ongoing encouragement and thoughtful feedback, Allison Bucknell for editing the manuscript and Jayanthi Sankar for guidance about book layout and final proof reading.

My family members in Singapore (who will feature in a future book) have been patient, kind and forgiving of my preoccupation with this book. I love you all.

Request

Thank you for reading my book.

If you enjoyed reading my story or found it useful, please leave a review on Amazon or Goodreads and share it on social media.

When I finished writing this memoir, I realised that the book was not an end but a beginning.

If you would like to join the ongoing discussion about divorce and receive support, please tune into Rewriting YOUR Happily Ever After podcast which begins where Rewriting MY Happily Ever After the book ends.

Whether you are thinking about, going through or finding your way after divorce, this podcast will help you rewrite your happily ever after.

If you would like to stay in touch, please connect with me through my website www.ranjanirao.com or signup for my newsletter.

If you know someone who needs to read this book, please let them know that they are not alone.

If you would like to share your story of divorce and self-discovery with me, ask a question, or simply talk, please email me at hi@ranjanirao.com so I can set up a call.

Thank you,
Ranjani

Scan the above QR code to visit my website.

www.ingramcontent.com/pod-product-compliance
Lightning Source LLC
Chambersburg PA
CBHW020519080526
44583CB00013B/659